A Church
DIVIDED

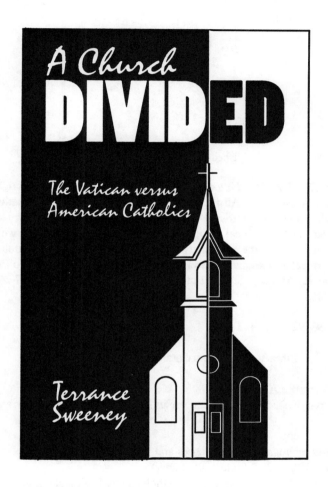

A Church
DIVIDED

The Vatican versus American Catholics

Terrance Sweeney

Prometheus Books • *Buffalo, New York*

Published 1992 by Prometheus Books

96 95 94 93 92   5 4 3 2 1

Library of Congress Cataloging-in-Publication Data

Sweeney, Terrance A.
    A church divided : The Vatican versus American Catholics / Terrance
Sweeney.
        p.   cm.
    Includes bibliographical references and index.
    ISBN 0-87975-735-3 (hard : alk. paper)
    1. Catholic Church—Clergy. 2. Catholic Church—Teaching office. I. Title.
BX1912.S79   1992   92-3672
262′.142—dc20   CIP

Printed in the United States of America on acid-free paper.

To my wife
Pamela
and to my brother
Patrick—
in so peacefully facing death
he taught me the meaning of courage

Acknowledgments

There are many people whose assistance and support made this book possible.

I wish to thank those who offered to read and critique parts of or all of this manuscript, among them: Dr. Karl-Josef Kuschel and Professor Hans Kung of the Institute for Ecumenical Studies at the University of Tubingen; Fr. Charles Curran; Ms. Mona Moore and Ms. Barbara Clow; Professor Philip Bonacich of the Sociology Department, University of California, Los Angeles; Fr. Joseph H. Fichter, S.J., Department of Sociology, Loyola University of New Orleans; Fr. Roger de Ganck and his Cistercian Community of Our Lady of the Redwoods Monastery in Whitehorn, California; and Fr. John L. McKenzie, of happy memory. Even though their views and those expressed in this book were not always in agreement, they were most thoughtful and helpful in their suggestions.

Because the sociological data in this book proved to be extremely controversial, the Church imposed official sanctions abrogating my vows of obedience, celibacy, and poverty, separating me from the

Jesuit Order, and suspending my canonical ministry as a Catholic priest. Throughout these events, friends and family members supported me, and thereby exposed themselves to the criticisms intended for me. I am deeply grateful to these people, among whom are: Grace and George Fritzinger, Tom and Sheila McDonald, Dr. Milton and Betsy Heifitz, Gregory and Veronique Peck, Fr. Ellwood Kieser, Susan Stafford, Dan Enright, Sr. Marie O'Connor, Jimmy Hawkins, Rosa V. Witt, Jeanette Reynolds, Bob and Jackie Marlin, Gerald Sullivan, Jeanne and Robert Sully, the Prietto family, Dana and Cubby Broccoli, the Melanson family, Fr. Ernest Sweeney, Gregg and Theresa Maday, John Leira, Rick Flynn, Edward Daneri, the Reverends Peter Krietler and Gregory Richards, Bishop Daniel Corrigan, Dr. and Mrs. William Bergin, Dr. Stephen Shoop, the Sweeney family, and Rupert Allan.

I am grateful to Maria and Barney Landgraf, to David Rejl and Emil Svrcina for their computer assistance with the priestly ministry survey data, and to Eugene O'Connor for editing this manuscript.

Also, I would like to thank Gary Bostwick and Jane Wolf Eldridge of Bostwick & Ackerman for their legal counsel, and Professor Lawrence Tribe of Harvard University for his opinion on whether the canons requiring celibacy for priests stand in violation of the U.S. Constitution.

Lastly, I wish to express my indebtedness to Fr. James Coriden of the Washington Theological Union for helping to prepare my formal appeal to the Apostolic Signatura and to the Sacred Congregation for Clergy in Rome in order to determine whether Cardinal Mahony had superceded his authority and that of canon law in banning me from Communion.

Contents

9

List of Abbreviations
of Ecclesiastical Sources

ACO   *Acta conciliorum oecumenicorum.* Edited by E. Schwartz. Berlin and Leipzig, 1927ff.

CC   *Corpus Christianorum: Series latina.* Belgium: Turnhout, 1954ff.

CSEL   *Corpus scriptorum ecclesiasticorum latinorum.* Vienna, 1866ff.

DS   H. Denzinger, *Enchiridion symbolorum, definitionum et declarationum de rebus fidei et morum.* Edited by A. Schonmetzer. New York, 1963.

DV2   *Documents of Vatican II.* Edited by W. Abbott and J. Gallagher. New York: Guild Press, 1966.

Mansi   *Sacrorum conciliorum nova et amplissima collectio.* Edited by J. D. Mansi. 31 vols. Florence, 1759–1798; Paris, 1901ff.

MGH   *Monumenta Germaniae historica.* Edited by G. H. Pertz, T. Mommsen, et al. Berlin, Hannover, Leipzig, et al., 1826ff.

NCE   *New Catholic Encyclopedia.* New York: McGraw-Hill, 1969.

NPNF   *Nicene and Post-Nicene Fathers.* Edited by P. Schaff and F. Wace. 2 series, 14 vols. each. New York, 1886–1890, 1890–1900.

PG   *Patrologia graeca.* Edited by J. P. Migne. 161 vols. Paris: Garnier Fratres, 1857–1886.

PL   *Patrologia latina.* Edited by J. P. Migne. 221 vols. Paris: Garnier Fratres, 1844–1864.

Prologue

"Every kingdom divided against itself is heading for ruin and a household divided against itself collapses."

> *Jesus' reply to the religious leaders who said his power over evil spirits came from the devil (see Luke 11:14–22; Mt. 12:22–29; Mk. 3:22–27)*

The Roman Catholic Church, the largest organized religion in the world, claiming a membership of over 900,000,000 people, is divided.

We can point to many signs of this division. During the close of the 1990 worldwide Synod on Priestly Formation, the pope thanked the Synod for "unequivocally confirming" priestly celibacy; but at the same time a survey of the North American hierarchy found that, of those responding, 68 percent of the Canadian bishops and 32 percent of the U.S. bishops would approve "changing the current practice so that priests would be able to choose either celibacy or marriage."

Traditionalist archbishop Marcel Lefèbvre, shortly before his death, was excommunicated in the very act of consecrating four bishops. Immediately after his excommunication, the Vatican issued both an invitation and a warning to the followers of the archbishop: Either return to the authority of the pope, who would give special attention to the Traditionalists' concerns that the reforms of Vatican II had diverted the Church from its spiritual and liturgical heritage, or be excommunicated along with the archbishop.

In 1986, the Catholic University of America, following a directive from the Vatican, stripped Fr. Charles Curran of his teaching position as professor of moral theology after he presented a moral perspective on homosexuality, premarital sex, birth control, and other sexual issues that were at variance, in specific cases, with the official teaching of the Catholic hierarchy. This action, amidst the protest of theologians and professors nationwide, resulted in a lawsuit against the university.

The visit of Pope John Paul II to the United States in the fall of 1987, while demonstrating his immense personal appeal and a vibrant American Church, proved beyond doubt that large numbers of Catholics—over 90 percent—believe they can disagree with the pope and still be good Catholics. And disagree they do. A nationwide poll conducted by *Time* magazine in August 1987 revealed that, despite the official teaching of the Church enunciated in the papal encyclical, *Humanae Vitae,* only 24 percent of Catholics believe artificial birth control is wrong, while 76 percent believe divorced Catholics should be allowed to remarry and 53 percent believe priests should be allowed to marry. In a *Los Angeles Times* nationwide poll, published August 23, 1987, 65 percent of the respondents felt it was "wrong" to exclude women from the clergy; and only 14 percent believed that the pope is "infallible."

Responding to American Catholics' widespread disagreement with many of the Church's teachings, the Vatican has emphasized that the Church "is a theocratic institution, not a democratic one." Vatican officials have warned the U.S. faithful against falling into a "pick-and-choose Catholicism," and reminded them, "It is not possible to disagree with Church teaching and still be a good Catholic."

And while the current pope is the most widely traveled and the most visible in the Church's history, and while his proclamations of faith and his social doctrine founded on the God-given dignity of the human person are respected the world over, there is ever-increasing complaint and dissatisfaction expressed over the way authority is exercised in the Church, over the way women are relegated to secondary roles, and over the silencing of intelligent dissent. There has been vehement objection to the fact that, in the 1988 Synod on the Laity, not one lay person out of nearly 900,000,000 had a vote in any of the policy statements affecting the future of the laity.

Since Vatican II, over 19,000 priests in the United States, and over 100,000 worldwide, have "resigned" the priesthood. The economic fallout from these resignations is staggering. Using the extremely conservative figure of $15,000 per year for the eight years of diocesan training, it is estimated that resignations of American clergy would have cost the Church over $2 billion, while resignations worldwide would have cost over $12 billion. And this expense refers only to the training of those seminarians who persevered the eight years to ordination. The emotional and spiritual trauma accompanying these resignations and their impact on the faithful is immeasurable.

At the same time that women are demanding an equal role in all ministries in the Church, including the priesthood, over 60,000 nuns in the United States and 300,000 worldwide have left their convents. Irrational accusations are hurled at these women, charging them with everything from caving in to the "me-ism" of the age to penis envy. Prelates denying equality are called sexists, misogynists, or men whose judgment has been vitiated by clericalism and patriarchy.

These divisions have become serious enough to generate continual questions about the possibility of schism, and the possibility of the American Church and other national conferences breaking off from the authority of Rome. However real this might prove to be, it is far more telling to realize that already there exists a massive "psychological schism" from many of the teachings proclaimed by the Vatican.

Many Catholics today assert that the "Church is the people of God," and that the hierarchy are "out of touch with real life." And even though the institutional Church disclaims them—because of their sexual mores, or divorces, or practice of birth control, or public dissent from "official teaching"—these Catholics are claiming the Church. They are demanding more participation in shaping the future direction of their Church, more freedom, and more justice and equality. There appears to be large numbers of faithful who have internalized the Church's teachings on social justice, as well as on the freedom and dignity of every person. And they have directed those very teachings not only to the world at large, but to the Church's own internal structures. Women are boldly asserting God's invitation to them to become priests. Priests are marrying publicly, without dispensation from Rome, and continuing to practice their ministry in spite of the canon laws forbidding them. And while the majority of U.S. Catholics would favor a married clergy and women priests, Rome decries such notions and actions as deceptions and scandals.

Many Catholics have learned the difference between dogma and discipline, between God-given commandments and man-made rules. They have learned that faith is their responsibility as well as Rome's, and they will not have religion dictated to them by decree or by appeals to the ultimate dialogue-silencer, "infallibility."

In the maelstrom of complaints and demands surrounding the current exercise of authority in the Church, these fundamental questions must be answered: What is authority? Who has it? How is it verified? Clearly, a church divided against itself cannot stand. History has proven this clearly enough with the break between the Jews and the Jewish Christians; the Catholic Church of Rome and the Catholic Church of Constantinople; Martin Luther and the Protestant Reformation; and Henry VIII's definitive separation of the Catholic Church in England from the supremacy of the pope.

The divisions now plaguing the Catholic Church are deep-rooted and destructive. This book focuses on two issues that stand at the very core of this crisis: authority and the priesthood. Part One of this book presents a sociological analysis of the division that exists between Church policy and the attitudes of Catholic laity, priests, and bishops on the issues of the ordination of women and a married priesthood. Part Two explores further the issues of married clergy, women priests, and ecclesiastical authority. From biblical, historical, canonical, and pastoral perspectives, this Part demonstrates the far-reaching consequences of an authority improperly conceived and exercised. Part Three presents the author's views on an authority that emanates from the properly ordered instincts of human nature.

More specifically, this book explores whether the hierarchical and infallible model of authority now operative in the Church is the authority Jesus intended. Further, this book, through questions relating specifically to the issues of married and women priests, examines whether the current Vatican policy forbidding both is consonant with the spirit of Christ.

Jesus was able to strip away the sanctimonious forms of authority and discipleship in his day. He saw through the hypocrisy of the Pharisees, the jealousy of his apostles, and the cultural subjugation of women. He knew that authority was not coterminus with office, nor was worth inherently determined by gender. He knew that what counted were faith and love, not gender and power. This is why Jesus chose women as well as men to proclaim his gospel, and why he constantly reminded his apostles that the "least among you will be the greatest—the first last. . . ." This is why Jesus called Peter "Satan" the moment Peter tried to stand in the way of God's will, and why he warned Pilate: "You would have no power over me were it not given you from above." This is why Jesus was able, even in his greatest anguish and abandonment, to cry out: "Father, into your hands I commend my spirit." But today, 2,000 years after that cry of total sacrifice, it must be asked whether the authority of the Church continues to reflect that spirit.

Part One

Priestly Ministry:

A Sociological Analysis of the Division Between Church Policy and Church Attitudes

Introduction

In his January 25, 1983 promulgation of the revised Code of Canon Law, Pope John Paul II said, "We, therefore, exhort all our beloved children to observe, with sincere mind and ready will, the precepts laid down. . . ."

But there are particular canons within that body of Church law that appear to be a source of disagreement and conflict. These canons concern the exclusion of women and married men from the priesthood. According to Church law, only baptized males can "validly receive sacred ordination" (canon 1024). Also, according to Church law, men who want to become priests must first promise that they will not marry (canon 1037); those who have been ordained are obliged to "observe perfect and perpetual continence" (canon 277.1); "those who are in sacred orders invalidly attempt marriage" (canon 1087); and any "cleric who attempts marriage, even if only civilly, incurs a *latae sententiae* suspension.* If, after warning, he has not reformed

---

*I.e., automatic suspension, in contrast to a suspension that takes place only after a formal judgment (*sententia*) has been brought against the one purportedly violating the canon.

and continues to give scandal, he can be progressively punished by deprivations, or even by dismissal from the clerical state" (canon 1394.1).

The ministry of priests is one of the primary ways by which the Gospel of Jesus is proclaimed to the world. Massive departures from that priesthood, or a substantial decline in the number of persons entering seminaries, merit serious consideration. Statistical data regarding the numbers of priests and seminarians from 1965 to 1990 demonstrate both massive departures and a substantial decline. In addition, sociological surveys conducted from 1966 through 1986 indicate that the majority of Catholic priests and laity would prefer a priesthood that encompasses both celibacy and marriage, men and women.

Those advocating a change in the current discipline cite many reasons: that the laws are a man-made discipline, not justifiable on New Testament grounds; that they are a slight to human freedom, to the married state, and to the dignity of women; that they are burdensome, and a vehicle for maintaining control over priests and over the wealth of the Church; and that they are an obstruction to the proclamation of the Gospel.

Vatican response to these objections has included exhortations to priests to be faithful to their celibate witness as a sign of the Resurrection and of special commitment and availability to the Church. Women are reminded that there were no women among the Twelve, and that "Jesus was and remains a man." During papal visitations and at the close of the 1990 Synod on Priestly Formation, Pope John Paul II emphasized that the possibilities of ordaining women or allowing priests to marry "are not to be taken into consideration."

This Part consists chiefly of a three-part sociological study. Following a summary of the events motivating this survey on priestly ministers, chapter 2 shows results from a 1985 survey of U.S. bishops' attitudes on the ordination of women and on the acceptance of a married priesthood. Chapter 3 presents the results of a 1990 survey of U.S. and Canadian bishops' attitudes on the same two issues. Chapter 4 is a comparative study of eleven different surveys, spanning the years 1966 through 1990, which report the attitudes of U.S. Catholic laity, priests, and bishops on the same issues.

Within one month of the time the 1985 survey was mailed out to 312 U.S. bishops and 122 cardinals worldwide, this researcher was ordered under "holy obedience," with the threat of expulsion from his religious order and suspension from the priesthood, to "cease and desist all work on this project, and destroy everything you have gathered." At the time this directive was handed down from the Superior General of the Jesuit Order in Rome, no conclusion, written or otherwise, regarding the bishops' responses to the survey had been reached.

Considering it wrong, however, to suppress the attitudes of the American bishops and the cardinals worldwide, this researcher made a formal appeal to the Vatican's Sacred Congregation for Religious to determine whether the Vatican judged the directive consonant with "holy obedience." The Vatican Congregation replied that the directive should have been obeyed "just as if it were coming from Christ our Savior. . . ."

Among other conclusions, this sociological data and Rome's efforts to suppress it demonstrate four things. First, regarding the "Church's" policy excluding women and marriage from the priesthood, substantial numbers of laity, priests, and bishops do not assent to this policy "with sincere mind and ready will." Second, many bishops think that "Christ's teachings, the mission of the Church, and the pastoral needs of the faithful" would be better served by changing the current policy. Third, the Vatican Congregation for Religious considers it consonant with the spirit of Christ to suppress the minds of the American bishops and cardinals throughout the world. Fourth, in the actual exercise of Vatican authority in relation to the current priesthood policy, the power of "primacy," even in merely disciplinary matters, takes precedence over the pastoral needs of the faithful, the mission of the Church, and Christ's teachings.

1

Events Motivating This Study on Priestly Ministers

" 'It is you who say it,' answered Jesus. 'Yes, I am a king. I was born for this, I came into the world for this: to bear witness to the truth; and all who are on the side of truth listen to my voice.'
" 'Truth?' said Pilate, 'What is that?' "

John 18:37–38

INTRODUCTION

Since Vatican II, over 100,000 priests in the Roman Catholic Church have resigned the priesthood.[1] Given the fact that, worldwide, there are some 400,000 priests,[2] the departure of so large a number in slightly more than twenty years has been the source of serious concern.[3] This concern focuses not only on the motives for priests' departure, but also on the effects this is having and will continue

24

to have on the spiritual life of the Catholic Church, with the consequent limiting or closing of missions, schools, and churches.

Compounding this serious concern over departure is the substantial decline in the number of people enrolling in seminaries. Based on data gathered by the United States Center of Applied Research in the Apostolate during the years 1968 to 1983, seminary enrollment at the high school and college levels declined 74 percent, at religious novitiates 68 percent, and at theologates 50 percent.[4]

This substantial decline in the United States Catholic seminary enrollment is especially noteworthy in light of three research discoveries:

1) In a comparison of U.S. Catholic and Protestant seminary enrollment, it was found that between 1969 and 1982, the total enrollment in Masters of Divinity and Bachelors of Divinity programs (the principal study programs leading to ordained ministry) increased 33.4 percent in the member schools of the Association of Theological Schools.[5]

2) The strongest obstacle for Catholic men considering a vocation to the priesthood is that they are "not allowed to marry";[6] and, if "married men could be ordained, the number of men desiring ordination would increase, as an estimate, fourfold or more."[7]

3) "If women could be ordained, the number of women desiring some form of vocation would increase twofold or more."[8]

STRESS AND THE DECLINE OF PRIESTS

North America has the highest ratio of priests per Catholics, one per 991; even so, 10 percent of the U.S. parishes do not have a resident priest. In 1987, 24 percent of Canadian priests were sixty-five or older, and only 26 percent were under fifty. In their report to the 1990 Synod on Priestly Formation, the Canadian bishops said, "If these trends continue, it can be expected that ten years from now, less than 15 percent of the priests will be under fifty years of age."

The U.S. bishops sponsored a study directed by Richard Schoenherr titled, "The Catholic Priest in the U.S." The study projects a 40 percent decline in the number of diocesan priests between 1966 and 2005; during that same period, the Catholic population will increase by about 36 percent. In 1990, there was one priest per 2,000 Catholics; by the year 2005, the ratio will be one priest per 3,100 Catholics. Elsewhere, the statistics are even more grim. In Africa in 1988, there was one priest per 4,249 Catholics. In that same year, in South America, there was one priest per 7,014 Catholics. Worldwide, 43 percent of parishes do not have a resident pastor.

As the priest-per-Catholic ratio declines, increased responsibilities and burdens are placed on the shoulders of remaining priests and bishops. A 1988 report from the U.S. National Conference of Catholic Bishops revealed that priests, as a result of being overworked, sexually troubled, and lonely, were suffering from a "substantial morale problem." The report went on to say that mandatory celibacy was cited as a major reason for loneliness, and for resignation from the priesthood.

During the June 1990 meeting of U.S. Catholic bishops—in the wake of requests by several bishops (including Hunthausen, Quinn, Marino, Welsh, and Gerber) for special leaves to deal with exhaustion and stress-related problems—a keynote address was given by Jesuit psychiatrist James Gill on the subject of balancing the stressful demands of the episcopacy with attentiveness to personal growth.

The direct relationship between the declining numbers of priests per Catholics and increased levels of stress underscores the urgency of finding solutions to the priesthood shortage.

PASTORAL URGENCY AND VATICAN POLICY

While Catholic priests and laity are asking, with increasing frequency, for a change in the current discipline, the Vatican has repeatedly said no to the possibility of married priests and women deacons or priests.[9] This presents a dilemma for the bishops, who, on the one hand, owe loyalty to the Holy See and to the discipline of the Church, but on the other, are obligated to minister to the needs of their people. When there is a direct conflict between the two, how is the bishop to choose?[10] And why?

The 1990 worldwide Synod on Priestly Formation illustrates this conflict. Prior to the synod, the Vatican sent out to all the bishops a discussion paper on priestly formation. The Canadian bishops drafted a document that was sharply critical of Vatican attitudes on the priesthood. Among other criticisms, the Canadian document stated:

> The Vatican's view of the priesthood "lacks vision and dynamism; it views the situation with a haughty eye and fails to ask honest and in-depth questions about the dramatic decrease in the number of priests. It also leaves little place for contemporary questions such as limited terms for the priest, celibacy, the ordination of married men, and the ordination of women."
>
> The Vatican document displays a "harsh attitude towards contemporary society and emphasizes only the negative aspect of Western society. Democracy, the religious and political freedom of Western culture, and its economic and technological ingenuity are positive values which the Church should celebrate. Instead, the outline wants to protect priests from the hard realities of the modern world."
>
> The Vatican outline reflects an old-fashioned view of the priesthood. "The ministry of the bishops is centered more on power than on sensitive service in the midst of the people."

During the 1990 synod, the papally appointed recording secretary, responsible for giving direction to the synod discussions, informed the delegates that they should concentrate on strengthening spiritual formation rather than arguing over priestly celibacy, ordaining women, or assigning ministerial tasks to laicized married priests.[11] In spite of this guideline, Bishop Valfredo Bernardo Tepe of Brazil called for the ordination of married men, and Cardinal Lorscheider of Brazil reminded the synod that in recent years two married men in Brazil had been ordained with Vatican approval.

At the synod's close, Pope John Paul II said: "The synod has unequivocally confirmed the choice of priestly celibacy. . . . Some people have asked if it wouldn't be possible in some circumstances to consider the ordination of mature married men of proven Christian virtue. This solution is not to be taken into consideration."

MANDATORY CELIBACY NOT WELL OBSERVED

There is increasing evidence that celibacy, when vowed not as a free and wholehearted choice but solely as a requirement for the priesthood, is not well observed.

According to Jeffrey Anderson, an attorney specializing in Church-related pedophilia cases, such cases have cost the Church in the U.S. over $100,000,000. In Canada, Archbishop Penney of Newfoundland resigned after a Church commission sternly reprimanded him for not taking action against the thirty priests, ex-priests, and religious brothers who were charged with molesting altar boys, orphans, and other children.[12]

Richard Sipe's book *A Secret World: Sexuality and the Search for Celibacy* estimates that at any given time, 50 percent of priests practice celibacy, while 50 percent do not. Of those who practice celibacy, Sipe maintains that only 2 percent have achieved celibacy in a "mature sense," while another 6 to 8 percent closely approximate the spirit of celibate love.

David Rice's book *Shattered Vows: Priests Who Leave* indicates that 80 percent of local priests in Peru live with women; that between 60 and 70 percent of native Brazilian priests are intimately involved with women; and that 50 percent of the priests in the Philippines live with women.

MANDATORY CELIBACY: ETHICAL CONSIDERATIONS

One of the two married priests Cardinal Lorscheider referred to during the 1990 synod is Fr. Ivo Schmitt. Fr. Schmitt and his wife,

Adulina, were married in 1947. Ivo was ordained in May of 1987. As a condition of her husband's ordination, Mrs. Schmitt had to sign a document giving up her rights as a wife, and Mr. Schmitt had to sign a document promising that, if he was ordained, he and his wife would "sleep in separate beds."

The Vatican insistence on the Schmitts' formally renouncing their marriage rights as a condition for ordination raises the following questions:

- Was such a requirement a violation of the marriage bond?

- Was such a requirement a violation of Christ's will: "What God has joined, let no man divide?"

- Was such a requirement a violation of God's commandment: "Thou shalt not covet thy neighbor's wife?"

- Is the right to marry a God-given, inalienable human right?

- Does the Church have the "authority" to impose either celibacy or marriage as a condition of the priesthood?

- Are laws that require either celibacy or marriage as a condition of the priesthood unethical?

These questions and the events alluded to above are far too complex to be analyzed in this sociological study of the American bishops' attitudes regarding married and women priests. They are mentioned here only to make note of the principal events and questions motivating this inquiry, and to suggest the timeliness and urgency of honestly and courageously addressing that model of hierarchical authority which allows its priesthood to be threatened by decline, stress, divided loyalties, scandal, hypocrisy, economic waste, and ethical ambiguity.

THE PURPOSE OF THIS STUDY

Catholic laity, priests, and bishops have been discussing a variety of ways to address the issue of priestly ministry. Chapters 2 and 3 of this volume, comprising the only poll of its kind to be directed exclusively to bishops, is intended to complement this discussion.

Hierarchical authority expects adherence "with sincere mind and ready will" to the canonical discipline of the Church and to the mind of the Holy See. This study, from a sociological analysis, will demonstrate whether the current discipline excluding marriage and women from the priesthood is accepted by laity, priests, and bishops with "sincere mind and ready will."

METHOD, CONTENT, AND PERSONS SURVEYED

The remainder of Part One consists of three surveys. The first (chapter 2) is a four-question poll of 323 U.S. bishops and 122 cardinals worldwide[13] on their attitudes concerning women's ordination and married priests. Initiated in November 1985, this poll was conducted by mail by this researcher. The responses of the U.S. bishops were then tabulated according to:

a) overall responses and usable responses

b) responses according to each of the four questions

c) responses according to each of the four questions and each of the four age categories: 40–49, 50–59, 60–69, and 70–79

d) responses according to each of the four questions and each of the four regions of the country: West, Midwest, South, and East

e) responses compared by question and by age category

f) responses compared by question and by region category.

A survey initiated by this researcher in April 1990 (chapter 3) expands the scope of the 1985 poll, both in terms of the number of questions asked and of the number of bishops surveyed. The number of questions pertaining to married clergy and women priests increased from four to seven. The 1990 poll, also conducted by mail, was sent to 363 U.S. bishops and to 84 Canadian bishops.

By tabulating the responses to this poll, and by comparing them with responses to the same questions asked in the 1985 poll, it was possible more fully to understand the following:

1) what percentage difference there is, over a five-year period, in the U.S. bishops' attitudes on married priests and women priests.

2) what percentage of North American bishops responding would approve of a priesthood that included married priests.

3) what percentage of North American bishops responding would approve of ordaining women to the diaconate or priesthood.

4) between the Canadian and the U.S. bishops responding to the 1990 poll, what percentage difference there is regarding their attitudes on married clergy and the ordination of women.

5) whether Vatican efforts to limit discussion of these issues is reflected in the response rate of bishops to polls on these issues.

The third survey (chapter 4) is a comparative study of data from twelve different surveys on the same four questions concerning priestly ministry. This comparison, based on data spanning twenty-five years and examining attitudes of various Catholic laity, priests, and bishops, is intended to compare and contrast attitudinal trends regarding priestly ministry.

LIMITATIONS OF THIS REPORT

Practical applications of the social sciences in such things as political polls, Nielsen ratings,[14] and corporate advertising demographics have enormous impact on the shaping and expression of culture. Nevertheless, all sociological reports, indeed all scientific investigations, have imitations. Such is the human condition, with limitations deriving from the cognitive capacity of the investigator; the act of knowing itself; and the complex nature of the matter, any matter whatsoever, under investigation.

This survey of the attitudes of Catholics on priestly ministry is likewise subject not only to the generic limitations of the "human condition" but also to the specific limitations deriving from attempting to ascertain in eleven surveys spanning twenty-five years, the attitudes of 55 million U.S. Catholics on the priesthood. It is a known fact that attitudes about specific issues change or stay the same, depending on the person, and his or her particular psychological and cultural milieu. With all the progress in the social sciences, there is still no incontestable formula for determining human attitudes or their changes. Apparently, cultures are not built on such formulas, but on decisions based on the knowledge at hand, limited though it may be.

In this perspective, therefore, surveys are accepted not as absolutes, but as indicators. As indicators, though, their potential for astute decision making, more effective communication, more profitable marketing campaigns, and directing successful political campaigns is enormous. This is so even in the face of the long-standing objection to demographic research: the opinions of a few can never accurately represent the opinions of all.

Social scientists, in particular, and the designers of demographic studies, polls, and surveys are fully aware of this objection. For this reason, they are constantly refining methods of audience selection (persons surveyed). Survey results are most often accompanied by a "caution" to the reader in the form of sampling error, or probability of error, which estimates the level of inaccuracy that might be found in a particular survey, directed to a particular sampling of people and purporting to express the mind of a much larger number of people.

This concept of sampling error does not apply to chapters 2 and 3 of Part One, since all[15] the North American bishops were surveyed, and their attitudes were not intended as a sampling of a larger group (such as the attitudes of Catholic bishops worldwide). This notion of sampling error does, however, apply to chapter 4, in terms both of the sampling error deriving from each of eight separate surveys and of the estimated sampling error in cross-comparing data from the eleven specific surveys cited.[16]

The surveys cited in chapter 4 are as valid as their specific method, content, and persons surveyed. The cross-comparison of these surveys is as valid as the specific comparison and contrast of the surveys' methods, contents, and persons surveyed. There are enough specific points of comparison in the surveys' methods, questions asked, and categories of persons surveyed to conclude both logical and mathematical continuity.

The function of sociological investigation is twofold: it provides information concerning specific social factors and it facilitates decisions impacting on specific social factors. Sociological investigation need not include both levels, but its pragmatic potential is best realized when it does. This report might not facilitate any decisions regarding priestly ministers—indeed, it has been suggested by one bishop in Los Angeles that given the current attitude of the pope and the "structure" of the Church, even if the majority of Catholic laity, priests, and bishops wanted changes in the current policy concerning priestly ministers, it would still not happen.[17] But whether a Church is governed "theocratically" or "democratically," governance itself is threatened with collapse when most of the governed disagree with a policy.

Finally, close to one month after the 1985 poll had begun, the Superior General of the Jesuit Order and the Jesuit Provincial of the California Province ordered this researcher to "cease, desist, and destroy" all data he had gathered from the U.S. bishops and the cardinals worldwide. This action, apparently prompted by pressure from the Vatican, raises serious questions not only about religious and academic freedom in the Catholic Church, but, more importantly, about the kind of "authority" that prompts someone to feel he has the right and the power to suppress the minds and attitudes of the college of cardinals and the American bishops.

NOTES

1. From the years 1963 to 1984, according to the "Annuarium Statisticum Ecclesiae," 46,302 priests have been dismissed from the priesthood. According to a September 4, 1985 article in the *New York Times,* "anywhere from 70,000 to 100,000 priests have gotten married in the two decades since Vatican II." In the September 6, 1985 issue of the *National Catholic Reporter,* the following item appeared: "Worldwide, about 125,000 priests have resigned since 1965."

2. The exact number given in the *1990 Catholic Almanac* is 402,243. Felician A. Foy, ed., *1990 Catholic Almanac* (Huntington, Ind.: Our Sunday Visitor, Inc.), p. 767.

3. This is especially evidenced by the following: the June 1986 meeting of 259 U.S. bishops in Collegeville, Minnesota, to discuss the shortage of vocations; the Dean R. Hoge five-part study of future Church leadership; Richard Schoenherr and Annemette Sorensen's "Decline and Change in the U.S. Catholic Church, from the Second Vatican to the Second Millennium"; the work of the National Opinion Research Center (NORC), particularly "The Catholic Priest in the United States: Sociological Investigations"; and the Center for Applied Research in the Apostolate Studies' *U.S. Catholic Institutions for the Training of Candidates for the Priesthood; Planning for the Future: Catholic Theology Schools, Formation Houses 1975–1983; A Statistical Report on Seminarians and Religious in Initial Formation.*

4. Dean R. Hoge, Raymond H. Potvin, and Kathleen M. Ferry, *Men's Vocations to the Priesthood and the Religious Life* (Washington, D.C.: Catholic University of America, 1984), p. 5.

5. Ibid., p. 18.

6. Ibid., p. 49.

7. Dean R. Hoge, *Report 1, Study of Future Church Leadership* (Washington, D.C.: Catholic University of America, 1986), p. 22.

8. Ibid.

9. During the 1987 papal visit to the United States, while numerous polls conducted across the country revealed that a majority of Catholics wanted a priesthood that would include marriage and women, Pope John Paul II reminded American Catholics that the "Church is a theocratic institution, not a democratic one," and that the current policy would remain unchanged.

10. Bishop William McManus maintains that a predominant stress

on bishops is that American Catholics and the Vatican are pulling them in opposite directions. Hans Kung commented on this tension between Vatican policy and pastoral responsibility: "The bishops are in a difficult situation, because they have pressure from below and above. But the gospel criterion is that the bishops have to stay not with the superior shepherds, but with the sheep. I am convinced that if just one bishop, but better six bishops of the U.S. episcopal conference, would say publicly what they think of the present situation (the priest shortage, Rome's authoritarian style, the erosion of the Eucharistic center) and not hide their opinions any more, things would change considerably."

11. This spirit stands in stark contrast to that of the 1971 Synod on the Priesthood. During that synod, 87 of the 194 bishops voted in favor of ordaining married men as priests, and Cardinal Arns of Brazil said, "Paul VI personally assured me that if the synod vote had been positive, he would have carried it out."

12. While announcing his resignation, Archbishop Penney said, "We are a sinful church. We are naked. Our anger, our pain, our anguish, our shame, and our vulnerability are clear to the whole world. I'm prepared to take the responsibility, and that's something I have to live with."

13. The list of cardinals was taken from the 1985 U.S. Catholic Directory, and the list of bishops was taken from the *1985 U.S. Catholic Directory* and the *1985 Catholic Almanac*. The overall response rate of the cardinals was 18 percent while the usable response rate was 8 percent. Three different sociologists advised that this response was too low to serve as a basis for sociological conclusions. Hence, the cardinals' responses have been excluded from this report.

14. For example, Nielsen ratings are a critical factor in determining which television programs stay on the air, and millions of dollars of advertising revenues depend on fractions of national ratings points.

15. That is, all those whose addresses could be found in the *1985 U.S. Catholic Directory* and the *1985 Catholic Almanac*.

16. Cross-comparing eleven different surveys spanning twenty-five years is possible thematically, but determining sampling error would be very complex.

17. During this Holy Saturday 1986 conversation, this researcher asked the bishop whether the Church was the community of the faithful guided by God and the Spirit of truth, or a "structure" guided by opinion.

2

Attitudes of U.S. Catholic Bishops Regarding Married Priests and the Ordination of Women (1985)

DATE OF MAILING, CONTENT, AND PERSONS SURVEYED

In November 1985, this researcher mailed a cover letter (see Attachment A1, Sample Letter) and survey on priestly ministers (see Attachment B1) to 323 U.S. bishops and 122 cardinals throughout the world.

SURVEY RESPONSE

As of April 10, 1986, 145 of the 312* bishops polled had responded to the survey. This represents a 46.4 percent response rate.

---

*Four letters to various bishops were returned unopened; two bishops had become cardinals; and five computer numbers of the total 323 were unassigned, thus reducing the total number of bishops polled to 312. Also, seven bishops wrote letters explaining why they would not answer the survey. Thus, the overall response rate of the bishops was 48.7 percent, while the usable response rate was 46.4 percent. Responses cited in this survey are in reference to the usable responses.

Bishops' Overall Responses, by Question, to the Survey

	Percentage of Total Responses	
	Approve	**Not Approve**

1) Optional celibacy for priests.

   Thirty-five bishops would approve, while 109 would not.   24.3%   75.7%

2) Inviting married and resigned clergy to return to active ministry.

   Twenty-seven bishops would approve, while 118 would not.   18.6%   81.4%

3) Ordaining women to the diaconate.

   Twenty-nine bishops would approve, while 98 would not.   28.5%   71.5%

4) Ordaining women to the priesthood.

   Eleven bishops would approve, while 133 would not.   7.6%   92.4%

**Bishops' Responses, by Question and by Age Category
(Ages 40-49)**

	Percentage of Total Responses	
	Approve	**Not Approve**
1) Optional celibacy for priests.		
Four bishops would approve, while five would not.	44.4%	55.6%
2) Inviting married and resigned clergy to return to active ministry.		
One bishop would approve, while seven would not.	12.5%	87.5%
3) Ordaining women to the diaconate.		
Five bishops would approve, while four would not.	55.5%	44.5%
4) Ordaining women to the priesthood.		
One bishop would approve, while eight would not.	11.1%	88.9%

**Bishops' Responses, by Question and by Age Category
(Ages 50-59)**

	Percentage of Total Responses	
	Approve	**Not Approve**
1) Optional celibacy for priests.		
Ten bishops would approve, while 37 would not.	21.2%	78.8%
2) Inviting married and resigned clergy to return to active ministry.		
Eight bishops would approve, while 39 would not.	17.0%	83.0%
3) Ordaining women to the diaconate.		
Twelve bishops would approve, while 34 would not.	26.0%	74.0%
4) Ordaining women to the priesthood.		
Three bishops would approve, while 44 would not.	6.3%	93.7%

Bishops' Responses, by Question and by Age Category (Ages 60-69)

	Percentage of Total Responses	
	Approve	**Not Approve**
1) Optional celibacy for priests.		
Sixteen bishops would approve, while 42 would not.	27.5%	72.5%
2) Inviting married and resigned clergy to return to active ministry.		
Fourteen bishops would approve, while 45 would not.	23.7%	76.3%
3) Ordaining women to the diaconate.		
Seventeen bishops would approve, while 37 would not.	31.4%	68.6%
4) Ordaining women to the priesthood.		
Five bishops would approve, while 52 would not.	8.7%	91.3%

Bishops' Responses, by Question and by Age Category (Ages 70-79)

	Percentage of Total Responses	
	Approve	**Not Approve**
1) Optional celibacy for priests.		
Three bishops would approve, while 21 would not.	12.5%	87.5%
2) Inviting married and resigned clergy to return to active ministry.		
Three bishops would approve, while 22 would not.	12.0%	88.0%
3) Ordaining women to the diaconate.		
Four bishops would approve, while 19 would not.	17.3%	82.7%
4) Ordaining women to the priesthood.		
One bishop would approve, while 24 would not.	4.0%	96.0%

Bishops' Responses, by Question and by Region (The West)

	Percentage of Total Responses	
	Approve	**Not Approve**

1) Optional celibacy for priests.

   Five bishops would approve, while 15 would not.   25.0%   75.0%

2) Inviting married and resigned clergy to return to active ministry.

   Four bishops would approve, while 15 would not.   21.0%   79.0%

3) Ordaining women to the diaconate.

   Eight bishops would approve, while 11 would not.   42.1%   57.9%

4) Ordaining women to the priesthood.

   One bishop would approve, while 19 would not.   5.0%   95.0%

Bishops' Responses, by Question and by Region (The Midwest)

	Percentage of Total Responses	
	Approve	**Not Approve**

1) Optional celibacy for priests.

   Fourteen bishops would approve, while 31 would not. — 31.1% — 68.9%

2) Inviting married and resigned clergy to return to active ministry.

   Eleven bishops would approve, while 36 would not. — 23.4% — 76.6%

3) Ordaining women to the diaconate.

   Seventeen bishops would approve, while 25 would not. — 40.4% — 59.6%

4) Ordaining women to the priesthood.

   Five bishops would approve, while 40 would not. — 11.1% — 88.9%

Bishops' Responses, by Question and by Region (The South)

	Percentage of Total Responses	
	Approve	**Not Approve**

1) Optional celibacy for priests.

   Eight bishops would approve, while 21 would not.   27.5%   72.5%

2) Inviting married and resigned clergy to return to active ministry.

   Nine bishops would approve, while 21 would not.   30.0%   70.0%

3) Ordaining women to the diaconate.

   Nine bishops would approve, while 19 would not.   32.1%   67.9%

4) Ordaining women to the priesthood.

   Five bishops would approve, while 25 would not.   16.6%   83.4%

Bishops' Responses, by Question and by Region (The East)

	Percentage of Total Responses	
	Approve	**Not Approve**
1) Optional celibacy for priests.		
Eight bishops would approve, while 40 would not.	16.6%	83.4%
2) Inviting married and resigned clergy to return to active ministry.		
Three bishops would approve, while 44 would not.	6.3%	93.7%
3) Ordaining women to the diaconate.		
Five bishops would approve, while 41 would not.	10.8%	89.2%
4) Ordaining women to the priesthood.		
No bishops would approve, while 47 would not.	0.0%	100%

Percentage of Bishops, Compared by Question and by Age Category, Who Would Approve

		Percentage of Total Responses			
Ages:	40-49	50-59	60-69	70-79

1) Optional celibacy for priests.

   In the four age categories, 4, 10, 16, and 3 bishops, respectively, would approve. 44.4% 21.2% 27.5% 12.5%

2) Inviting married and resigned clergy to return to active ministry.

   In the four age categories, 1, 8, 14, and 3 bishops, respectively, would approve. 12.5% 17.0% 23.7% 12.0%

3) Ordaining women to the diaconate.

   In the four age categories, 5, 12, 17, and 4 bishops, respectively, would approve. 55.5% 26.0% 31.4% 17.3%

4) Ordaining women to the priesthood.

   In the four age categories, 1, 3, 5, and 1 bishop(s), respectively, would approve. 11.1% 6.3% 8.7% 4.0%

Percentage of Bishops, Compared by Question and by Region Category, Who Would Approve

	Percentage of Total Responses			
Region:	West	Mid-west	South	East

1) Optional celibacy for priests.

In the four region categories, 4, 14, 8, and 8 bishops, respectively, would approve.	25.0%	31.1%	27.5%	16.6%

2) Inviting married and resigned clergy to return to active ministry.

In the four region categories, 4, 11, 9, and 3 bishops, respectively, would approve.	21.0%	23.4%	30.0%	6.3%

3) Ordaining women to the diaconate.

In the four region categories, 8, 17, 9, and 5 bishops, respectively, would approve.	42.1%	40.4%	32.1%	10.8%

4) Ordaining women to the priesthood.

In the four region categories, 1, 5, 5, and 0 bishops, respectively, would approve.	5.0%	11.1%	16.6%	0.0%

CONCLUSIONS

Data gathered from this 1985–1986 poll lead to the following conclusions:

"In light of the mission of the Church and the pastoral needs of the faithful"—

Of those bishops responding to the survey:

1) Nearly 25 percent of U.S. bishops would approve optional celibacy for priests.

2) Close to 20 percent of U.S. bishops would approve inviting married and resigned clergy to return to active ministry.

3) Close to 30 percent of U.S. bishops would approve ordaining women to the diaconate.

4) Nearly 8 percent of U.S. bishops would approve ordaining women to the priesthood.

5) Nearly 45 percent of U.S. bishops between the ages of 40 and 49 would approve optional celibacy for priests, while only 12 percent of U.S. bishops between the ages of 70-79 would approve.

6) Close to 25 percent of U.S. bishops between the ages of 60 and 69 would approve inviting married and resigned clergy to return to active ministry, while only 12 percent of U.S. bishops between the ages of 70 and 79 would approve.

7) Over 55 percent of U.S. bishops between the ages of 40 and 49 would approve ordaining women to the diaconate, while 17 percent of U.S. bishops between the ages of 70 and 79 would approve.

8) Eleven percent of U.S. bishops between the ages of 40 and 49 would approve ordaining women to the priesthood, while 4 percent of U.S. bishops between the ages of 70 and 79 would approve.

9) Over 30 percent of U.S. bishops in the Midwest would approve optional celibacy for priests, while 16 percent of U.S. bishops in the East would approve.

10) Thirty percent of U.S. bishops in the South would approve inviting married and resigned clergy to return to active ministry, while 6 percent in the East would approve.

11) Forty-two percent of U.S. bishops in the West would approve ordaining women to the diaconate, while 10 percent of U.S. bishops in the East would approve.

12) Sixteen percent of U.S. bishops in the South would approve ordaining women to the priesthood, while 0 percent of U.S. bishops in the East would approve.

13) Regarding four specific areas of the Catholic Church's current policy on priestly ministers:
   a) mandatory celibacy for priests,
   b) the exclusion of married and resigned clergy from active ministry,
   c) the exclusion of women from the diaconate,
   d) the exclusion of women from the priesthood,
      in none of these areas do the U.S. biships unanimously adhere with "sincere mind and ready will" to the current discipline.

14) The Church's "current policy" fails to address the pastoral needs of the faithful and the mission of the Church as perceived by:
   a) nearly 25 percent of U.S. bishops with regard to optional celibacy for priests,
   b) close to 20 percent of U.S. bishops with regard to inviting married and resigned clergy to return to active ministry,
   c) close to 30 percent of U.S. bishops with regard to ordaining women to the diaconate,
   d) nearly 8 percent of U.S. bishops with regard to ordaining women to the priesthood.

FURTHER ISSUES AND QUESTIONS
RAISED BY THIS SURVEY

The Superior General of the Jesuit Order ordered this researcher to "cease, desist, and destroy," all data gathered in connection with this survey. When he appealed to the Sacred Congregation for Religious the directive to suppress the data, this researcher was informed that the directive was appropriate because "the Holy See's position" had been clearly expressed on these issues.

The implication of this judgment is that the "mind of the Holy See" has authority over the minds of the U.S. bishops and the cardinals throughout the world. This hierarchical exercise of authority demonstrates that even in non-infallibly defined issues, the "Holy See's position takes precedence over the rest of the Church. Though, in fact, a significant portion of U.S. bishops would approve changes in the "current policy" regarding priestly ministers, the policy stands. This means, for those bishops and their dioceses, not only the subordination to the "current policy" of their attitudes on priestly ministers, but also the suppression of what they perceive to be the mission of the Church and the pastoral needs of the faithful.

The results of this survey, and the suppression of its data, raise the following crucial questions:

- What in the "current policy" is so vital as to take precedence over the mission of the Church and the pastoral needs of the faithful?

- Is this kind of hierarchical "authority" beneficial or detrimental to the Catholic Church?

- Why would the Holy See not want bishops freely and openly to discuss their attitudes on the vital issue of priestly ministry?

- Should the "current policy" take precedence over the mission of the Church and the pastoral needs of the faithful?

- Should the "current policy" be changed in such a way as to address the mission of the Church and the pastoral needs of the faithful as perceived by bishops who conclude that changes are needed?

- If the "current policy" representing the "international Church" directly conflicts with the "local Church's" mission and pastoral needs, which must take preference?

- If, in fact, the "current policy" fails to address the pastoral needs of the faithful and the mission of the Church on both the international and local levels, what does this say about the "current policy"?

- According to the current exercise of hierarchical authority, it is the responsibility and authority of the mind of the Holy See to determine whether the current discipline will be discussed or changed. Is this exercise of authority the kind of authority Jesus intended?

ATTACHMENT A1: SAMPLE LETTER

THE JESUIT COMMUNITY
LOYOLA MARYMOUNT UNIVERSITY

November 12, 1985

Most Reverend J. Keith Symons
Diocese of Pensacola/Tallah.
P.O. Box 106
Largo, FL 33540

Your Excellency: Greetings and Peace

I am writing this letter to you in an effort to further important research
on the timely issue of priestly ministry.

As you are fully aware, priestly ministry is a vital extension of the
mission entrusted by Jesus to his disciples. When priestly ministry is
seriously threatened, the mission of the Church suffers. According to the
"Annuarium Statisticum Ecclesiae", there are 404,459 priests worldwide in
1984. According to the same source, from the years 1963 to 1984, 46,302
priests have been dismissed from the priesthood.

According to a September 4, 1985 article in the New York Times, "anywhere
from 70,000 to 100,000 priests have gotten married over the two decades
since the Second Vatican Council ended".

In the September 6, 1985 issue of the National Catholic Reporter it
stated: "Worldwide, about 125,000 priests have resigned since 1965."
This means that well over 25% of the total, worldwide number of priests
have resigned the priesthood. From sociological, psychological, and
ecclesial perspectives, this constitutes a crisis.

The March, 1984 "News Notes" from the National Federation of Priests'
Councils in the United States says: "At its zenith in 1970, the diocesan
priesthood in the United States numbered some 37,000. By the year 2000,
it is estimated that this population will be 16,000 to 17,000. This would
represent a decline of some 54%...by the year 2000, those who are 56-75
years of age will account for almost half of the diocesan priests...
Another way of describing the phenomenon is that in the year 2000 we will
have roughly the same number of priests we had in 1925. Meanwhile, the
people we were ordained to serve will have quadrupled."

To date, surveys in both the United States and in Europe have indicated a
substantial majority of priests and laity in favor of optional celibacy.
To my knowledge, no such survey has been directed to the Hierarchy. That
is the specific purpose of this letter.

I would greatly appreciate it is you would take a few moments and respond
to the enclosed survey.

Entreating your prayers and blessing, I remain Your Brother in the Lord —

Fr. Terry Sweeney, Ph.D.

Post Office Box 45041   Los Angeles. California 90045   (213) 642-2700 642-3170

ATTACHMENT B1

The Jesuit Community
Loyola Marymount University

SURVEY ON PRIESTLY MINISTERS

Kindly mark an (x) in the appropriate space.

Please return the completed survey in the enclosed envelope.

In light of the mission of the Church and the pastoral needs of the faithful, I would:

1. Approve ____
              OPTIONAL CELIBACY FOR PRIESTS
    Not Approve ____

2. Approve ____
              INVITING MARRIED AND RESIGNED PRIESTS TO
              RETURN TO ACTIVE MINISTRY
    Not Approve ____

3. Approve ____
              ORDAINING WOMEN TO THE DIACONATE
    Not Approve ____

4. Approve ____
              ORDAINING WOMEN TO THE PRIESTHOOD
    Not Approve ____

Thank you for your time and consideration. And may the Lord continue to bless you with wisdom and grace in the care of His people.

In Domino,

Terry Sweeney

Fr. Terry Sweeney, Ph.D.

Post Office Box 45041   Los Angeles California 90045   213 642-3170

3

Attitudes of U.S. and Canadian Catholic Bishops Regarding Married Priests and the Ordination of Women (1990)

BACKGROUND

In 1970 and 1985, surveys containing questions about allowing a married priesthood and/or allowing women priests were sent to the U.S. bishops.[1]

In a 1970 NORC (National Opinion Research Center) survey, there were two questions pertaining to the issue of married priests: one question concerned whether the bishops would approve of optional celibacy for priests; the second, whether the bishops would approve of inviting married and resigned clergy to return to active ministry.

In the 1985 survey, conducted by this researcher (see chapter 2), there were four questions concerning, respectively, whether the bishops would approve of optional celibacy; if they would approve of inviting married and resigned clergy to return to active ministry; if the bishops would approve of ordaining women to the diaconate; and whether they would approve of ordaining women to the priesthood.

While the Vatican made no effort to suppress data from the 1970 survey, there was an attempt to suppress data from the 1985 poll. This fact, coupled with several other Vatican actions indicating that dissent under this pontificate would not be tolerated, prompted this researcher to wonder if the bishops would subsequently be more hesitant in discussing the current discipline regarding the priesthood.

A survey conducted by this researcher in 1990 (Attachment D1) expands the scope of the two previous surveys, both in the number of questions asked and of bishops surveyed. The number of questions pertaining to married clergy and women priests increased from four to seven.[2] To the four questions in the 1985 survey, the following three were added, namely, whether the bishops would approve:

- ordaining married deacons to the priesthood;

- maintaining the current practice of requiring, by law, priests to be celibate; and

- changing the current practice so that priests, by law, would be required to marry.

This 1990 survey is the most extensive yet conducted on the attitudes of North American bishops regarding the inclusion of marriage and women into the structure of the Roman Catholic priesthood. By tabulating the responses to this survey, and by comparing them with responses to the same questions asked in the 1970 and 1985 surveys, it is possible to obtain a more thorough overview of American bishops' attitudes on priestly ministry during the last twenty years.

LIMITATIONS

In none of the three surveys was there a 100 percent response rate from the bishops. In fact, the response rate varies substantially. Possible reasons for this difference are found in note 3. It is important to state here that the survey results presented below, particularly for the 1985 and 1990 surveys, should not be interpreted as revealing the attitudes of the entire body of Canadian and U.S. bishops.

In a time when information on these issues has become increasingly difficult to gather, the data presented below are meant to be a narrative and a record only of those bishops who did respond.

1990 SURVEY OF U.S AND CANADIAN BISHOPS ON PRIESTLY MINISTERS

The responses of U.S. and Canadian bishops to the survey questions are tabulated as follows:

	U.S. Approve	Canada Approve
1) In the absence of priests or deacons, training more lay persons to preside over Sunday liturgies.	86% = 48 of 56 respondents	96% = 24 of 25 respondents
2) In the absence of priests or deacons, delegating lay persons to solemnize marriages, baptize, and preside over graveside services.	81% = 47 of 58 respondents	88% = 22 of 25 respondents
3) Inviting priests from countries with an abundance of vocations to minister to the faithful's sacramental needs in our country.	71% = 41 of 58 respondents	74% = 17 of 23 respondents
4) Ordaining married deacons to the priesthood.	35% = 19 of 55 respondents	44% = 11 of 25 respondents
5) Maintaining the current practice of requiring, by law, priests to be celibate.	74% = 39 of 53 respondents	42% = 10 of 24 respondents
6) Changing the current practice so that priests, by law, would be required to marry.	2% = 1 of 57 respondents	4% = 1 of 25 respondents

1990 SURVEY (cont.)

	U.S. Approve	Canada Approve
7) Changing the current practice so that priests would be able to choose either celibacy or marriage.	32% = 18 of 56 respondents	68% = 17 of 25 respondents
8) Ordaining women to the diaconate.	40% = 23 of 58 respondents	59% = 13 of 22 respondents
9) Ordaining women to the priesthood.	14% = 8 of 57 respondents	36% = 8 of 22 respondents
10) Allowing local churches to elect their own bishops.	14% = 8 of 57 respondents	14% = 3 of 22 respondents
11) Asking married and resigned clergy to return to active ministry.	25% = 14 of 56 respondents	38% = 9 of 24 respondents

Thus we may note, between the U.S. and the Canadian bishops, a 13 percent variance on the first question; a 7 percent variance on the second; a 3 percent variance on the third; a 9 percent variance on the fourth; a 32 percent variance on the fifth; a 2 percent variance on the sixth; a 36 percent variance on the seventh; a 19 percent variance on the eighth; a 22 percent variance on the ninth; a 0 percent variance on the tenth; and a 13 percent variance on the eleventh.

CHANGES IN THE RESPONSE RATE OF U.S. CATHOLIC BISHOPS TO THREE SURVEYS ON PRIESTLY MINISTERS CONDUCTED OVER A TWENTY-YEAR PERIOD

In 1969–1970, NORC mailed out a questionnaire to all 276 U.S. bishops. Included in that survey were questions involving optional celibacy for priests, and inviting married and resigned clergy to return to active ministry. 163 of the 276 bishops polled responded to the survey, making a response rate of 59 percent.

In November 1985, this researcher mailed out a cover letter and survey to 312 U.S. bishops. 145 of whom responded to the survey, making a 46 percent response rate.

In April 1990, this researcher mailed out a five-year follow-up study, consisting of a cover letter and survey (see Attachments C1 and D1) to 363 U.S. bishops, 58 of whom responded to the survey, making a 16 percent response rate.

Thus, in the twenty-year period between 1970 and 1990, there was an overall decline in the response rate of 43 percent. In the fifteen-year period between 1970 and 1985, there was a 13 percent decline in the response rate; while in the five-year period from, 1985 to 1990, there was a 30 percent decline in the response rate.[3]

CHANGES IN THE ATTITUDES OF U.S. CATHOLIC BISHOPS ON PRIESTLY MINISTERS AS REFLECTED IN THE THREE SURVEYS

The following table offers a comparison of the U.S. bishops' responses in the three surveys to those questions regarding a priesthood that would include celibate and married, male and female priests.

	1970 Survey Approve	1985 Survey Approve	1990 Survey Approve
1) Optional celibacy for priests.	11%	24.3%	32%
2) Asking married and resigned clergy to return to active ministry.	9%	18.6%	25%
3) Ordaining women to the diaconate.		28.5%	40%
4) Ordaining women to the priesthood.		7.6%	14%
5) Requiring priests, by law, to be celibate.			74%
6) Requiring priests, by law, to be married.			2%

CONCLUSIONS

Based on data from this 1990 survey, the following conclusions can be drawn.

Regarding a Married Priesthood

Of those bishops responding:

1) Seventy-four percent of U.S. bishops approve of the current policy of mandatory celibacy; 26 percent do not.

2) Only 42 percent of the Canadian bishops approve of mandatory celibacy; a substantial 58 percent do not.

3) Seventy-five percent of U.S. bishops agree with the current policy barring married and resigned clergy from returning to active ministry; 25 percent do not.

4) Sixty-two percent of Canadian bishops agree with the current policy barring married and resigned clergy from returning to active ministry; 38 percent do not.

5) Sixty-five percent of U.S. bishops approve of the current policy precluding the ordination of married deacons to the priesthood; 35 percent do not.

6) Fifty-six percent of Canadian bishops approve of the current policy precluding the ordination of married deacons to the priesthood; 44 percent do not.

7) Sixty-eight percent of the U.S. bishops agree with the current policy that bars priests from choosing either marriage or celibacy; 32 percent do not.

8) Only 32 percent of the Canadian bishops agree with the current policy that bars priests from choosing either marriage or celibacy; a substantial 68 percent do not.

9) Ninety-eight percent of U.S. bishops and 96 percent of Canadian bishops would not approve of requiring priests, by law, to marry. This warrants the question: Why, on the one hand, would so many bishops approve of mandating celibacy, but, on the other, almost unanimously reject mandating marriage? Does this not entail a philosophical, canonical, and pastoral contradiction? Does this not compel asking the question: Has any institution or person the authority to mandate either celibacy or marriage?

Regarding the Ordination of Women

Of those bishops responding:

1) Eighty-six percent of U.S. bishops approve of the current policy excluding women from the priesthood; 14 percent do not.

2) Sixty-four percent of Canadian bishops approve of the current policy excluding women from the priesthood; 36 percent do not.

3) Sixty percent of the U.S. bishops approve of the policy barring women from the diaconate; 40 percent do not.

4) Forty-one percent of the Canadian bishops approve of the policy barring women from the diaconate; 59 percent do not.

From this data, we may draw the following conclusions concerning the Church's current policy excluding both marriage and women from the priesthood:

- The North American bishops do not unnanimously support the current policy.

- There are significant numbers of bishops who do not assent to this policy "with sincere mind and ready will."

- The majority of Canadian respondents would approve of optional celibacy for priests, and ordaining women to the diaconate.

Regarding the Twenty-Year Trend in the Bishops' Response Rate and in Their Attitudes Regarding Priestly Ministers

It is evident from the substantial decline (43 percent) in the response rate that U.S. bishops are far less likely to respond to or discuss publicly their attitudes about including marriage and women into the priesthood.

Comparing 1990 with 1970, the percentage of U.S. bishops responding who would approve optional celibacy for priests has nearly tripled in two decades (from 11 percent to 32 percent); and the percentage of U.S. bishops responding who would approve asking married and resigned clergy to return to active ministry has risen from 9 percent to 25 percent.

In the five-year period from 1985 to 1990, the percentage of U.S. bishops who would approve ordaining women to the diaconate has jumped from 28 percent to 40 percent; and the percentage of U.S. bishops who would approve ordaining women to the priesthood has doubled from 7 percent to 14 percent.

NOTES

1. For additional details, see *The Catholic Priest in the United States; Sociological Investigations* (Washington, D.C.: The National Opinion Research Center, 1972), especially p. 328.

2. In their responses to the 1985–1986 survey, some bishops wrote out alternative solutions to the priesthood shortage. Their concerns were taken into consideration while determining additional questions for the 1990 survey.

3. The 43 percent decline in the response rate is substantial, particularly in light of the fact that in the fifteen-year period between 1970 and 1985, the decline rate was only 13 percent. This drastic decline warrants

some kind of explanation. Following are some of the factors that may have precipitated the decline:

1) Because Rome's attempt to suppress the 1985 survey on priestly ministers made national headlines in the summer of 1986, many of the U.S. bishops became aware of the Vatican's unwillingness to allow discussion on the issues of married and women priests.

2) The Vatican reprimand of Archbishop Hunthausen and the temporary suspension of his authority made the bishops aware of how far the Vatican was willing to go to assure that its policies were carried out.

3) The stripping of Fr. Curran's faculties as a theologian reminded U.S. bishops that orthodoxy in matters of morals was expected in Catholic universities. This action, the 1989 Cologne Declaration, and the Vatican's "Instruction on the Ecclesial Vocation of the Theologian" demonstrated the tension between Vatican policy and theological inquiry. The Instruction stated: "One cannot speak of a 'right to dissent' in the church inasmuch as the freedom of the act of faith is linked to the moral obligation to accept the truth which the interventions of the Magisterium intend to serve. . . . Even when the Magisterium does not intend to act 'definitively' but teaches a doctrine in order to aid a deeper understanding of revelation, make its contents explicit, recall a doctrine's conformity with the truths of the faith, or finally to guard against ideas incompatible with these same truths, a religious submission of will and intellect is called for."

4) In 1989, in preparation for the 1990 Synod on Priestly Formation, the Vatican sent out to the bishops a discussion paper which precluded the possibility of open and honest discussion on the issues of married priests and the ordination of women.

The above events, which may well have led to the 43 percent decline in the response rate, seem to indicate that the window opened by Pope John XXIII and the Second Vatican Council has now been closed and sealed shut.

ATTACHMENT C1: SAMPLE LETTER

CHRISTUS REDEMPTOR

Pastoral Research Center
13906 Ventura Blvd., #238 • Sherman Oaks, California 91423

Palm Sunday, 1990

Name
Diocese
Address

Your Excellency:

The historic meeting of Mikhail Gorbachev with His Holiness Pope John Paul II, the crumbling of the Berlin Wall, the massive political changes sweeping across Eastern Europe with their accompanying cries of freedom and democracy - all these events seem to accentuate the urgency and timeliness of Christ's mandate: "Go, therefore, and make disciples of all the nations, baptising them in the name of the Father and of the Son and of the Holy Spirit, and teach them to observe all the commands I gave you. And know that I am with you always; yes, to the end of time."

The 1990 World Synod on the Priesthood is coming at a time in which "restructuring" and "openness" are political attitudes allowing the most significantly positive changes since the birth of Socialism. The Synod, in its discussions and decisions regarding the Priesthood, has a unique opportunity to witness to the world that distinctive freedom promised by Christ: the freedom to know and to proclaim the truth, to celebrate and to live the Paschal Mystery, and to love one another as sons and daughters of God.

It is in this freedom, and guided by the Spirit, that the Synod can discern what forms priestly ministry should take to lead the Church into the 21st century. In listening to the voice of Christ as found in the hearts of all the faithful - laity, priests, and Bishops - the Synod can decide, with conviction and assent, what forms of ministry will best serve the people of God.

The task is not an easy one. Difficult questions face the priesthood, questions concerning not only mission, but also identity, and authority. For example: Where does priestly ministry originate - in the Pope? in the Twelve and their appointed successors? in the faithful responding to the call of Christ in their hearts? in governing bodies claiming power over priestly ministry?

The importance of carefully answering this question can be seen in the following tensions: various Church conferences are calling for a return to the practice of local Churches electing their own Bishops; the Chinese government, in fact, appoints its own Bishops; the Pope claims this authority belongs neither in the State, nor in the majority will of the faithful, but solely in the Vicar of Christ.

Which interpretation is more consonant with the mind of Christ? Why? How can this interpretation be best communicated so that universal harmony might be achieved?

ATTACHMENT C1: (CONTD.)

Another issue: Who has the right to decide marriage - the individual? or the institution? Canon Law in the Latin Rite requires Catholic priests to be celibate. The Government in China requires Catholic priests to marry. Are both right? Wrong? Why? What common truths and principles should be evoked to clarify this most delicate issue?

Because there were no women among the Twelve, and no women at the Last Supper, and because Jesus was a man, does this mean that He intended that no woman, ever, be the Celebrant of His Eucharistic Prayer? What can be said to those who claim this "exclusion of women" violates the intent of God's Spirit revealed in: Genesis 1:27; Galatians 3:27-28; Romans 16:1-5; Acts 9:1-5; Mark 3:31-35; John 17:20-23? And what might be said to those who ask: Did any of the Twelve more fully embody, consecrate, and reveal the Lord's Passion, Death, and Resurrection than his own Mother?

Since Vatican II, practically every major study on the policy precluding marriage and women from the priesthood indicates that this policy has become an ever-increasing source of consternation and distress. And this distress appears to have become even more acute when discussion itself is curtailed under the dictum: "Roma locuta est, causa finita est." If the long-repressed cries of freedom now struggling to reshape the very foundations of the Soviet Union tell us anything, it is that official silence does not prove consent - nor does prescribed dialogue or policy prove unity of minds or hearts.

Laity, priests, and citizens of good will the world over are looking to the Episcopacy as examples of discernment, justice, courage, honesty, and inspiration. Careful attention will be paid to your Synod, and to the freedom and principles with which you help shape the future of the priesthood.

Please be assured of our prayers as you prepare for this extremely important convocation. May the Spirit guide your hearts and minds.

Respectfully in the Lord,

Rev. Terrence A. Sweeney, Ph.D.

Research Director
Pastoral Research Center
Christus Redemptor

ATTACHMENT D1

CHRISTUS REDEMPTOR

Pastoral Research Center
13906 Ventura Blvd., #238 • Sherman Oaks, California 91423

This survey is part of a post Vatican II study of the attitudes of the Episcopacy on vital issues facing priestly ministry. Kindly reflect on the questions, mark your answer with an "X", and return the survey in the envelope provided.

IN THE LIGHT OF CHRIST'S TEACHINGS, AND THE SPIRIT OF GOD GUIDING CHURCH TRADITION AND THE HEARTS OF THE FAITHFUL, I WOULD:

1.   Approve ___   *in the absence of priests or deacons, training more*
       Not Approve ___   *lay persons to preside over Sunday liturgies.*

2.   Approve ___   *in the absence of priests or deacons, delegating lay*
       Not Approve ___   *persons to solemnize marriages, to baptize, and to preside over graveside services.*

3.   Approve ___   *inviting a sufficient number of priests from countries*
       Not Approve ___   *which have an abundance of vocations to minister to the Faithful's Sacramental needs in our country.*

4.   Approve ___   *ordaining married deacons to the priesthood.*
       Not Approve ___

5.   Approve ___   *maintaining the current practice of requiring, by law,*
       Not Approve ___   *priests to be celibate.*

6.   Approve ___   *changing the current practice so that priests, by law,*
       Not Approve ___   *would be required to marry.*

7.   Approve ___   *changing the current canons so that priests would be*
       Not Approve ___   *able to choose either celibacy or marriage.*

8.   Approve ___   *ordaining women to the diaconate.*
       Not Approve ___

9.   Approve ___   *ordaining women to the priesthood.*
       Not Approve ___

10.   Approve ___   *local Churches electing their own Bishops.*
       Not Approve ___

11.   Approve ___   *asking married and resigned clergy to return to active*
       Not Approve ___   *ministry.*

Thank You!

4

Attitudes of U.S. Catholic Laity, Priests, and Bishops Regarding Married Priests and the Ordination of Women (1966–1990)

The purpose of this portion of our survey on priestly ministers is to demonstrate whether the attitudes of Catholics (bishops, priests, and laity) on the issues of women's ordination and married clergy reveal acceptance of the current policy with "sincere mind and ready will." This will be achieved by presenting U.S. Catholic laity's, priests', and bishops' responses to eleven different surveys conducted over the last twenty-five years. The foundations for making this comparison are found in the questions themselves, in that they are identical or very similar, and also in the persons surveyed in that they are all part of the U.S. Catholic Church, and have been identified in one of three distinct categories (laity, priest, bishop) within the Church.

The twelve surveys and their specific questions pertaining to priestly ministers, which are included in this comparison, will now be cited.

1) Joseph H. Fichter's groundbreaking 1966 survey of U.S. priests showed that 62 percent of them would "be in favor of the diocesan's priest's freedom of choice to marry."[1]

2) The 1970 National Opinion Research Center (NORC) Study on the Catholic Priest in the United States showed that 11 percent of the U.S. bishops "agree strongly" or "agree somewhat" that "celibacy should be a matter of personal choice for diocesan priests"; and 9 percent of the U.S. bishops "agree strongly" or "agree somewhat" that "priests who have resigned from the priesthood should be invited to reapply for permission to function as priests again, whether they are married or single."[2]

3,6) The 1986 Report of Hoge, Shields, and Verdieck on the Attitudes of American Priests in 1970 and 1985 on the Church and Priesthood showed that 54 percent of all Catholic priests in 1970, and 53 percent in 1985, "agree strongly" or "agree somewhat" that "celibacy should be a matter of personal choice for diocesan priests"; and 51 percent of all Catholic priests in 1970, and 48 percent in 1985, "agree strongly" or "agree somewhat" that "priests who have resigned from the priesthood should be invited to reapply for permission to function as priests again, whether they are married or single."[3]

4) The Gallup Organization's 1983 Study of Attitudes of Roman Catholics Toward Permitting Priests to Marry showed 58 percent of Catholics would "favor allowing Catholic priests to marry and continue to function as priests."[4] And the Gallup Organization's 1982 Study of Attitudes of Roman Catholics Toward the Ordination of Women Priests showed that 44 percent of Catholics "agree it would be a good thing if women were allowed to be ordained as priests."[5]

5) The November 25, 1985 *New York Times*/CBS News Poll on The Views of American Catholics showed that

63 percent of Catholics "favor letting priests marry"; and 52 percent of Catholics "favor women as priests."[6]

7) The 1985 Sweeney Survey on the Attitudes of U.S. Bishops on Priestly Ministers shows that 24 percent of the bishops "would approve optional celibacy for priests"; 18 percent of the bishops "would approve inviting married and resigned clergy to return to active ministry"; 28 percent of the bishops "would approve ordaining women to the diaconate"; and 7 percent of the bishops "would approve ordaining women to the priesthood."[7]

8) The 1986 Report by Hoge, Shields, and Verdieck on the Attitudes of Priests, Adults, and College Students on Catholic Parish Life and Leadership showed that 63 percent of all Catholic priests "agree strongly" or "agree somewhat" that "it would be a good thing if married men were allowed to be ordained as priests"; 40 percent of all Catholic priests stated that it would "help" to "invite ex-priests who are currently married to become active parish priests again"; 43 percent of all Catholic priests stated that it would "help" to "open up the office of permanent deacon to women"; and 38 percent of all Catholic priests "agree strongly" or "agree somewhat" that "it would be a good thing if women were allowed to be ordained as priests."[8]

9) The 1986 Hoge, Shields, and Verdieck Report showed that 51 percent of college student leaders "agree strongly" or "agree somewhat" that "it would be a good thing if married men were allowed to be ordained as priests;" 31 percent of campus ministry student leaders stated that it would "help" to "invite ex-priests who are currently married to become active parish priests again"; 68 percent of campus ministry student leaders stated that it would "help" to "open up the office of permanent deacon to women"; and 49 percent of college student leaders "agree

strongly" or "agree somewhat" that "it would be a good thing if women were allowed to be ordained as priests."[9]

10) The same 1986 Report showed that 63 percent of all Catholic adults "agree strongly" or "agree somewhat" that "it would be a good thing if married men were allowed to be ordained as priests"; 48 percent of all Catholic adults stated that it would "help" to "invite ex-priests who are currently married to become active parish priests again"; 56 percent of all Catholic adults stated that it would "help" to "open up the office of permanent deacon to women"; and 47 percent of all Catholic adults "agree strongly" or "agree somewhat" that "it would be a good thing if women were allowed to be ordained as priests."[10]

11,12) The 1990 Sweeney Survey indicated that 32 percent of the U.S. bishops and 68 percent of the Canadian bishops "approve changing the current practice so that priests would be able to choose either celibacy or marriage"; 25 percent of the U.S. bishops and 38 percent of the Canadian bishops "approve asking married and resigned clergy to return to active ministry; 40 percent of U.S. bishops and 59 percent of Canadian bishops "approve ordaining women to the diaconate"; 14 percent of the U.S. bishops and 36 percent of the Canadian bishops "approve ordaining women to the priesthood."[11]

SUMMARY

Data gathered from the eleven different surveys cited above lead to the following conclusions regarding the current policy that excludes both marriage and women from the priesthood:

1) Neither the Canadian bishops nor the U.S. Catholic bishops, priests, or laity unanimously support the current Church policy.

2) Concerning the issue of the ordination of women as deacons, the majority of U.S. Catholic laity and Canadian bishops do not assent to the current policy "with sincere mind and ready will"; rather, they would prefer to see the policy changed to include the ordination of women as deacons.

3) The majority of U.S. Catholic laity would approve the ordination of women as priests.

4) The majority of U.S. Catholic laity, priests, and Canadian bishops would approve a priesthood that includes both marriage and celibacy.

5) While the majority of U.S. and Canadian bishops agree with the current policy of excluding women from the priesthood, and while the majority of U.S. bishops agree with the policy requiring priests to be celibate, there are significant numbers of U.S. and Canadian bishops who think that the inclusion of marriage and women into the priesthood would be more consonant with Christ's teachings, the mission of the Church, and the pastoral needs of the faithful.

FURTHER ISSUES RAISED BY THIS STUDY

In response to objections raised about the current policy, the pope has already stated, "The Church is a theocratic institution, not a democratic one." Apparently, this assertion is meant to imply that Church policy shall be shaped not by majority vote, but by God's will. But it is precisely at this level that the most serious difficulties arise. Those bishops wanting to see a change in the policy do so "in light of Christ's teachings, the mission of the Church, and the Spirit of God guiding Church tradition and the hearts of the faithful." Such attitudes are not merely an expression of opinion; they are choices based on theological and pastoral experience. When so many bishops disagree on this level with the current discipline, and are unable to change that discipline in their dioceses, the pastoral and theological implications are serious.

Here are but a few of those implications:

- Bishops, in their teaching, governing, and sanctifying roles are subject to the canonical discipline of the Church.

- Bishops, in matters of canonical discipline relating to mandatory celibacy and the exclusion of women from ordination, are subject to the power and the opinion of the Holy See.

- In those dioceses where the bishops would change the current policy, but have not done so, Christ's teachings, the mission of the Church, and the pastoral needs of the faithful are subject to the canonical discipline of the Church.

- The majority of Catholic laity, priests, and bishops, in their discernment of God's will, Christ's teachings, and the mission and needs of the Church, are subject to the canonical discipline of the Church and to the power of the Holy See.

- If Christ's will is one, and if hierarchical authority, through the assent "with sincere mind and ready will" of pope, bishops, and priests is a manifestation of that one will, the current division between priests, bishops, and pope over the current policy on the priesthood indicates either that Christ's will is divided, or that hierarchical authority is not a manifestation of Christ's will.

NOTES

1. Joseph H. Fichter, *America's Forgotten Priests* (New York: Harper & Row, New York, 1968), p. 163.

2. See *The Catholic Priest in the United States; Sociological Investigations* (Washington, D.C.: The National Opinion Research Center, 1972), p. 328.

3. Cf. Table 2, p. 3, in Report 4 of Hoge et al., *The Study of Future Church Leadership* (Washington, D.C.: Catholic University, 1986).

4. This 1983 Gallup study on permitting priests to marry was based on in-person interviews with 1,326 Roman Catholic adults in more than 330 scientifically selected locations.

5. For further details, see the Gallup Organization's "A Study of Attitudes of Roman Catholics Toward the Ordination of Women Priests: A Report to the Quixote Center," 1982.

6. These are part of a poll of 927 telephone respondents conducted November 18-19, 1985. For additional details, see the November 25, 1985, issue of the *New York Times*.

7. See chapter 2.

8. See Hoge et al., *The Study of Future Church Leadership,* pp. 2-3, Report 3, Tables 3 and 4.

9. Ibid., pp. 2-3.

10. Ibid., Tables 3 and 4

11. See chapter 2.

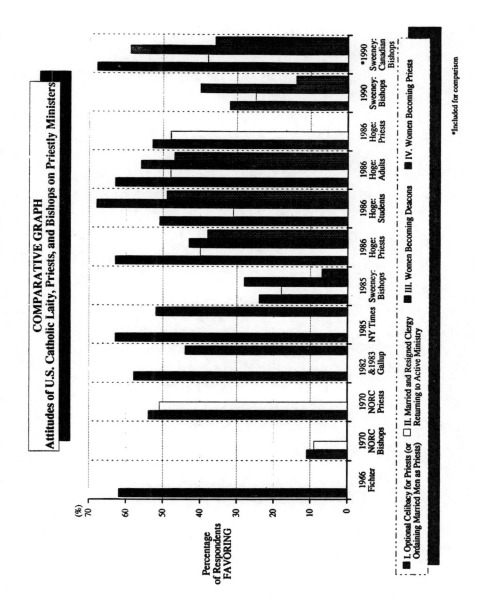

COMPARATIVE GRAPH
Attitudes of U.S. Catholic Laity, Priests, and Bishops on Priestly Ministers

Percentage
of Respondents
FAVORING

■ I. Optional Celibacy for Priests (or
   Ordaining Married Men as Priests)
□ II. Married and Resigned Clergy
   Returning to Active Ministry
■ III. Women Becoming Deacons
■ IV. Women Becoming Priests

*Included for comparison

Part Two

Celibacy, Sexism, and Infallibility:

Church Authority versus Divine Authority

Introduction

Part Two is concerned with ecclesial authority as currently defined in the matters of celibacy, women priests, and papal infallibility.

Some 1,700 years ago, under the newly-formed celibacy canons, married clergy were required, under threat of dismissal from the clerical state, to abstain from sexual intercourse with their wives. From the fourth century until the Second Lateran Council in 1139, some popes championed the continence and celibacy canons; others totally disregarded them, married, and fathered children.

The intent of chapter 5 is to examine in summary fashion the "discipline" of priestly celibacy and the "authority" that demands it. The central question of this chapter is whether laws mandating celibacy are valid. Does the "Church" indeed have the authority to demand, by law, celibacy of its priests?

Approaching this same question from an entirely different perspective might clarify its ethical and ecclesial importance: Suppose the pope were to enact a set of laws that would nullify all priestly promises of celibacy, and that would require all present and future priests to marry. Would not concerned bishops, priests, and laity consider such laws an affront to human dignity and inimical to the good of the Church? Would not such laws be decried as invalid and unethical? If, then, neither the pope nor the Church has the "authority" to command priests to marry, can either have the "authority" to command priests to be celibate?

Chapter 6 examines two arguments presented in the Vatican Declaration on "The Admission of Women to the Ministerial Priesthood" which purportedly support the exclusion of women from sacred ordination. The first argument maintains that, because "Jesus was and remains a man" and because sacraments must have a natural resemblance to what they signify, women cannot represent Christ in the Eucharistic consecration. The second asserts that, because Jesus called twelve men to be his apostles and because there were no women among these twelve, women, therefore, cannot receive the "apostolic charge."

Chapter 7 reviews the history of Church authority and examines whether it emanates directly from Jesus. This chapter shows how the doctrine of papal infallibility is inconsonant with the spirit of Jesus, who advocated a direct relationship with God, not one mediated by an ecclesial hierarchy that demands unquestioning obedience.

5

Married Clergy

"Thou shalt not covet thy neighbor's wife . . ."
                                        9th Commandment

"What God has united, man must not divide."
                                Jesus, in Mt. 19:1–9; Mk. 10:1–12

"Do we not have the right to be accompanied by a wife, like all the other apostles and the brothers of the Lord and Cephas?"
                                        St. Paul, 1 Cor. 9:5

The words of St. Paul[1] and the lives of the virgin-martyrs,[2] the desert fathers,[3] and many others throughout history bear inspiring testimony to the virtues of freely chosen celibacy[4] and continence.[5]

The purpose of this chapter is not to question the intrinsic virtue of continence or celibacy chosen and lived freely and lovingly; nor is it intended in any way to demean the promises and vows of those many nuns and priests who chose to dedicate their hearts to God and to the Church by remaining unmarried and chaste. Rather, this chapter examines a certain contradiction between Church teaching regarding marriage and Church laws regarding celibacy.

From its beginnings, Christianity has defended, as God-given, the marriage bond and its inviolability. Nonetheless, from the fourth century through the present, various popes, synods, and councils have enacted laws which, under threat of punishment, required:

- married priests not to have children;

- married priests to abstain from sexual intercourse with their wives;

- married priests to separate physically from their wives.

- married priests to divorce their wives;

- the valid marriages of priests to be decreed invalid;

- unmarried priests, and men wanting to become priests, to promise, as a condition of the priesthood, that they would never marry.

A few examples of these laws will now be cited.

Canon 33. "Bishops, presbyters, and deacons and all other clerics having a position in the ministry are ordered to abstain completely from their wives and not to have children. Whoever, in fact, does this, shall be expelled from the dignity of the clerical state." (ca. 305, during the Synod of Elvira)[6]

Canon 9. "We urge that priests and levites should not live with their wives." (386, Council of Rome)

Canon 9. "Furthermore what is right, chaste, and honorable, we urge that priests and levites do not have relations with their wives, because in the ministry they are occupied with the daily duties of their ministry. Paul wrote to the Corinthians: 'Abstain to be free for prayer.' If abstinence is prescribed for the laics in order that their prayer be heard, how much more ought the priest at every moment be prepared, tranquil with a purity without stain, lest he have to offer the sacrifice or baptize unwillingly. . . ." (418, Council of Africa)

Canon 22. "But if it is discovered that anyone, after having received the levitical blessing, has not kept continence with his spouse, he shall be dismissed from his functions." (441, Council of Orange)

Canon 2. "One is not to elevate to the priesthood a man entered into the bonds of marriage, if he does not first convert to continence." (442–506, 2nd Council of Arles)

Canon 17. "Priests and deacons are not to share the same bed or the same bedroom with their spouse, for fear that one might suspect them of carnal intercourse, and that their religious life would not be (unblemished). (If they do this), let them be deprived of their function, in conformity with the ancient canons." (541, Council of Orleans)

Canon 20. "If a priest, shameful to say, a deacon or a subdeacon, brings children into the world after having received the levitical blessing, or commits adultery, he shall not receive communion for an entire year." (561–605, Council of Auxerre)

Canon 21. "A priest, after having received the levitical blessing, is not permitted to sleep in the same bed with his spouse, nor to give himself over to sins of the flesh. . . ." (561–605, Council of Auxerre)

Canon 5. "We forbid absolutely the cohabitation with concubines or wives by priests, deacons, or subdeacons. If any of that kind, however, should be found, they are to be deprived of their offices and benefits. . . . Indeed, if they will not have corrected their filthy ways, they should be deprived of Christian communion." (1119, Council of Rheims)

Canon 7. "(For priests, deacons, subdeacons, canons regular, monks, and lay brothers) we sanction that copulation of this kind, which was contracted against ecclesiastical rule, is not matrimony." (1139, Lateran Council II)

Canon 9. "If anyone says that clerics in sacred orders or regulars who have made solemn profession of chastity can contract marriage, and that the one contracted is valid notwithstanding the ecclesiastical law or the vow, and that the contrary is nothing else than a condemnation of marriage, and that all who feel that they have not the gift of chastity, even though they have made such a vow, can contract marriage, let him be anathema. . . ." (1563, Council of Trent, Session XXIV)

Canon 2388.1. "Clerics in higher orders, and regulars or nuns with solemn vows of chastity, who presume to contract marriage, even though it be only a civil one, and all those who presume to contract such marriage with one of the aforesaid persons, incur excommunication. . . ." (1917)

Canon 132.1. "Clerics who are in major orders are prevented from marrying and are so bound to observe chastity that if they sin against it they are guilty also of sacrilege. . . ." (1917)

Canon 1087. "Those who are in sacred orders invalidly attempt marriage." (1983)

Canon 1037. A "candidate for the permanent diaconate who is not married, and likewise a candidate for the priesthood, is not to be admitted to the order of diaconate unless he has, in the prescribed rite, publicly before God and the church undertaken the obligation of celibacy. . . ." (1983)

Canon 277.1. "Clerics are obliged to observe perfect and perpetual continence for the sake of the kingdom of heaven, and are therefore bound to celibacy. Celibacy is a special gift of God by which sacred ministers can more easily remain close to Christ with an undivided heart, and can dedicate themselves more freely to the service of God and their neighbor." (1983)

Canon 1394.1. ". . . A cleric who attempts marriage, even if only civilly, incurs a *latae sententiae* suspension. If, after warning, he has not reformed and continues to give scandal, he can be progressively punished by deprivations, or even by dismissal from the clerical state." (1983)

Since these canons and the inviolability of the marriage bond stand in direct contradiction to one another, and since the Church teaches that these man-made laws are merely disciplinary, while marriage and its inviolability are established by God, it is necessary to ask:

- What factors motivated the formulation of such canons?

- What were some of the effects of these canons?

- Are canons that mandate continence for married clergy wrong?

- Are canons requiring celibacy as a condition of the priesthood wrong?

FACTORS MOTIVATING THE FORMULATION OF THE CONTINENCE AND CELIBACY CANONS

Though there were specific historical circumstances and personalities behind the promulgation of each of the celibacy canons, our purpose here is to give a brief summary of some of the most important factors that resulted in the formulation of the earliest canons.

The Life of Jesus

While the lack of any mention in the New Testament that Jesus had a wife has led many to conclude that he was unmarried, some have argued tht he was. The Jewish scholar Ben-Chorin offers a "chain of indirect proofs" that Jesus was married. Judaism in the time of Jesus regarded marriage as a fulfillment of God's commandment to "be fruitful and multiply." As Luke 2:51–52 points out, Jesus lived under the authority of his parents, and "grew in wisdom, stature, and favor before God and men." Ben-Chorin argues that in all probability Jesus' parents, as was the custom, sought out for him a suitable bride, and that Jesus, like every young man, especially those who studied the Torah, entered into the married state. Further, had Jesus not been married, he most certainly would have been reproached for this omission by those Pharisees who opposed him. Moreover, St. Paul, in presenting reasons supporting the value of celibacy, would undoubtedly have cited Jesus' own life, had Jesus been celibate. But St. Paul does not do this. For these and other reasons, Ben-Chorin concludes that Jesus was married.

Even though it would be interesting to know definitively from direct scriptural testimony whether Jesus was married or celibate, the fact is that in choosing disciples to proclaim the good news of salvation and the coming of God's reign, Jesus chose women and men, married and unmarried. In doing this, Jesus demonstrated that there was no intrinsic incompatibility between marriage and discipleship. Various sayings of Jesus have, over the centuries, been used to justify the requiring of celibacy for priests (Mt. 19:10–12, 27–30, 22:23–33; Mk. 10:28–31, 12:18–27; Lk. 9:57–62, 14:25–27, and 18:28–30); but Jesus did not choose the "Twelve" from the celibate Essene community, nor did he ask his married apostles to leave their families or practice continence with their wives. The "Follow me" call of Jesus to his disciples was an invitation to set the proclamation of the kingdom of God as the foremost priority in life.

Some have argued that Jesus' words, such as "For when they rise from the dead, men and women do not marry; no, they are like the angels in heaven," offer proof that celibacy is a way "more perfect" than marriage because it is a sign of the Resurrection. But those asserting this are implying that they know better than Jesus—who chose married apostles—how the gospel should be proclaimed. Jesus did not measure perfection by comparing states of life. Perfection was measured by faith and love; it was these that most revealed the reign of God.

After Jesus died, his disciples gathered together and "broke bread in his name," trying to discern what his life meant to them and to the rest of the world. St. Paul considered this "supper of the Lord" sacred, and warned against drunken or uncharitable conduct. As this memorial supper changed from a meal celebrated in homes to a ritual sacrifice offered over an altar, increasing emphasis was placed on the sacredness of the "bread and wine" as embodiments of Jesus' offering to God. As this cultic interpretation developed, more "purity" was required of the priest offering this sacrifice, since he was touching the "pure body and blood of the Lord." This concept obviously did not originate with Jesus, who associated closely with and loved even those who betrayed and abandoned him.

The Apostle Paul

At the time of his conversion, Paul was a Pharisee (Phil. 3:6), and, as such, had an unconditional duty to marry. Clement of Alexandria, writing in *Miscellanies* III, 53 (ca. A.D. 200) states that the apostle Paul was married, that he referred to his wife in Phil. 4:3, and that he defended his right to take her along with him on his missionary journeys (I Cor. 9:5). Even so, Paul was a firm supporter of the unmarried life and has been called the apostolic herald of celibacy. Some have even argued that Paul's "celibacy" was life-long and by divine mandate; therefore, those who carry on the apostolic mission must also be celibate. Such speculation, however, is far afield of Paul's own life and thinking.

In I Cor. 7, Paul distinguishes his personal opinion on celibacy and marriage from the Lord's will. Because of these "times of stress" and because the "world as we know it is passing away," Paul offers his opinion that it is "good for a man to stay as he is"—if married, to stay married; if celibate, to remain so. But "it is better to marry than to burn" (I Cor. 7:9).

Celibates, Paul suggests, are more free to devote themselves to the Lord, while the married are anxious about their spouses.[7] But he counseled married couples to honor one another's desire for intercourse, even if they did agree for a time to abstain from sex in order to be free for prayer; for they should come together again, lest Satan tempt them through lack of self-control.[8] Paul instructed Timothy and Titus to appoint "elders" (presbyters) who were of "irreproachable character" and "not married more than once" (I Tim. 3:2; Titus 1:6).[9]

Paul emphasized that it was the "Lord's will" that the wife should not separate from her husband, and that the husband should not divorce his wife (I Cor. 7:10). He also said that those who taught that marriage was forbidden were uttering the doctrine of demons (I Tim. 4:1–3).

Paul's praise of celibacy ran counter to the prevailing attitude of the Jewish community, who considered barrenness an opprobrium, and to the laws enacted by the emperor Augustus penalizing celibacy.[10] Although Paul's attitudes on celibacy, marriage, and conjugal abstinence were clearly stated, his name was unfairly invoked by those after him to justify "chaste marriages" (married couples mutually promising not to have sex), conjugal abstinence between priests and their wives, and priestly celibacy.

If, then, the notion of discipleship requiring celibacy originated neither with Jesus nor St. Paul, whence did it come?

Christian Beginnings: Identity and Survival

The first three centuries of Christianity can be characterized as a struggle for identity and survival. The early "followers of the Way" began proclaiming the teachings and miraculous deeds of Jesus of Nazareth, who had been crucified and had risen from the dead.[11] To most of the Jewish community, this was blasphemy, and to many in the Gentile world, foolishness. The early Christians were subjected to mockery, imprisonment, and martyrdom; but they gave such powerful witness to their faith that eventually Constantine decided that the empire would benefit considerably by recognizing Christianity as its religion. Until Constantine's Edict of Milan in A.D. 313, Christianity had been a religion without official recognition: it had been expelled from the synagogue and persecuted by Roman rulers. And it had to forge its own path through the pervasive influences of Gnosticism and Manichaeism.

Gnosticism

Gnosticism incorporated various religious and philosophical movements.[12] Although it predated Christianity, it readily assimilated some of Christianity's most attractive elements. Gnosticism's central teaching was dualistic: there were two worlds, one material and evil, the other spiritual and good. Human beings had both good and evil in them, and their purpose on this earth was to rid themselves of the evil of this world, and after death, return to their Creator. This was done through a saving gnosis (knowledge) that had been secretly revealed, and that could be transmitted to others only by those already initiated. The most effective way by which the Gnostic could assure escaping the bondage of the material world was the adoption of a stringent asceticism and sexual abstinence.

One of the most persuasive of the Gnostic leaders was Marcion, a Christian who was excommunicated in A.D. 144 from his Christian community in Rome. Marcionites regarded nature as evil, since it was created out of evil matter; and because they did not want to fill the earth with more evil, they abstained from marriage.[13] Marcion taught that Jesus had descended from heaven as a fully formed adult, without undergoing birth, boyhood, or temptation.[14] He allowed baptism and the Eucharist only to widows, virgins, and to married couples who agreed to refrain from sex.[15]

Julius Cassianus, also a Gnostic, claimed that men became most like beasts when they practiced sexual intercourse.[16] Jesus had come to earth to prevent men from copulating. Justin Martyr, a Neoplatonic dualistic philosopher who converted to Christianity, was so averse to sex that he could not imagine Mary as sexually conceiving Jesus; he argued, rather, that Mary must have conceived while still a virgin.[17] While not forbidding marriage, Justin affirmed that Christians should marry only for the purpose of conceiving and rearing children.[18] Justin's disciple, Tatian, who had a profound influence on the development of the Syrian Church, taught that sexual intercourse had been invented by the devil, and that even conjugal intercourse was evil.[19] Even though the early Church Fathers opposed Gnosticism, its impact was far-reaching. This is demonstrated by the fact that Tertullian, one of the most outspoken critics of Gnosticism, stopped just short of condemning conjugal intecourse, and wondered why God had ever permitted such an act.[20]

Manichaeism

The Manicheans were a new Christian sect founded on the teachings of the prophet Mani, who was crucified in southern Babylonia in A.D. 277. Manichaeanism included elements of Gnostic, Christian, Zoroastrian, and Greek teachings. It had a canonical scripture (the seven books of Mani) and a hierarchy that included apostles. Manichaeism basically taught that the universe was divided into two kingdoms, one of light, the other of darkness. Both light and darkness were eternal, uncreated, and in everlasting conflict. The conflict began when the prince of darkness invaded the kingdom of light. The father sent primordial man, a supernatural being of light, to fight against the king of darkness and his sons. Primordial man and his sons lost, and were devoured by their victors.

> To rescue Primordial Man the god of light sent forth his word or the Living Spirit, and after conquering the sons of Darkness, he created the earth, the moon, the sun, the planets, and man, all of which retained some elements of the darkness since, as materials, the God of light had used the carcasses of the defeated sons of Darkness.[21]

Since man contained elements of both light and darkness, his purpose was to rid himself of the darkness and to regain the light. Through the act of procreation, the spirit was kept prisoner in the dregs of material creation—sexual intercourse chained the soul to Satan. Thus, Manichaeism regarded marriage as a sin and procreation as impeding the kingdom of light. The human race was divided into three classes: the elect, who practiced celibacy, renounced private property, never engaged in trade, never drank wine, and were strictly vegetarian; the auditors, who were men and women of good will who served the elect and strove to be like them, but could not yet contain their desires (they owned property, married, and ate and drank what they craved); and the wicked, who were totally lost in their sensuousness, and who rejected the gospel of Mani. At death, the wicked were doomed to everlasting punishment in hell, while the auditors suffered a time of purification in purgatory; the elect enjoyed immediately the paradise of light.

For eleven years, Augustine strove to become a member of the Elect, but was unable to control his sexual desires.[22] Fathering a son with his mistress, and frustrated at his inability to control his lust, Augustine finally decided to marry. He sent away his mistress and his son, and became engaged to a girl merely twelve years old and hence not yet of legal age. Augustine found himself unable to wait for his betrothed; instead, he took a mistress. After this, his crisis of conscience became acute. Reading a passage from Romans resulted in his conversion to Christianity and acceptance of the life of celibacy.

Augustine carried his own struggle with sexuality into his Christian writings. He spoke of the "concupiscence" of Adam and Eve, a sexual impulse generated by the very act of their rebellion from God.[23] This lust was the strongest of human passions, and least obedient to the will. Nothing more brought "the manly mind down from the heights than a woman's caresses and that joining of the bodies without which one cannot have a wife."[24] Though conjugal intercourse as a procreative act was good since God willed it, all desires for the pleasures of coitus were evil, and thus, every child was thought to be conceived in the sin of his parents.[25]

Even though Augustine eventually opposed Manichaeism, and Christianity rejected Gnosticism, these two philosophical sects and their aversion to marriage and sexual intercourse had a far-reaching influence.

St. Gregory of Nyssa termed marriage a sad tragedy.[26] Tatian regarded sexual intercourse as an invention of the devil and felt that the Christian life was "unthinkable outside the bounds of virginity."[27] St. Ambrose thought of marriage as a "galling burden" and urged all those thinking of matrimony to consider the bondage and servitude of conjugal love.[28] Origen, who intimated that the vow of the Nazarene was one of perfect chastity,[29] castrated himself. Various Christian communities, not to be outdone by the ascetical zeal of pagan religions, tried to best them in all their forms of renunciation. A second-century medical writer, Galen, commented that the Christians in Rome included men and women who, like the philosophers, refrained from "cohabitating all through their lives."[30]

The Edict of Milan

By the time Christianity was recognized as the official religion of the empire, there were already strong advocates for a continent and celibate clergy. But the security of "official recognition" and the power, land, endowment, and wealth that came with it, added impetus to fashioning a clergy who would owe their loyalties to the "Church" rather than to their families, and who would own nothing donated to the "Church" except what had been bestowed on them by the bishop. Imperial recognition had a profound influence on the Church's perception of its own authority, as well as on its administrative structure.

Canon 33 of the Synod of Elvira was the first known canon that, under threat of dismissal from the clerical state, imposed continence on married bishops, presbyters, and deacons. The Council of Nicea of A.D. 325 tried to propose a similar canon, but it was rejected after the celibate Bishop Paphnutius,[31] who had suffered the loss of his right eye rather than recant his faith, argued that Jesus' words had made it clear that marriage was indissoluble. Later, in the West, Eusebius argued that priests should not give up their wives, only conjugal relations with them.[32] St. Ambrose added to Eusebius's notion that unmarried men at the time of their ordination should remain single because they would be celebrating the sacraments daily.[33]

Thus, by the middle of the fourth century, positions had been argued which favored: continuing the then-current practice of allowing the clergy to choose either marriage or celibacy; requiring, by law, that unmarried clergy promise never to marry; and requiring, again by law, that married clergy abstain from conjugal intercourse. Thus began a series of continence and celibacy canons that subsequently led the priesthood into seventeen centuries of conflict.

WHAT WERE SOME OF THE EFFECTS OF THE CELIBACY CANONS?

Countering papal efforts to impose continence on married clergy, the monk Jovinian taught, among other things, that the married state was equal to virginity.[34] He was branded as a heretic and driven out of Rome and Milan. When, later, his arguments supporting the virtue of marriage prompted some professed virgins to abandon their vow and marry, Jovinian was thrashed with a leaded thong and permanently exiled to he desolate rock of Boa.

In 742, under the auspices of Boniface and the Carolingian prince,

Carloman, a synod was held to reform the clergy, some of whom were marrying after entering the priesthood, which was prohibited; others, already married, were not practicing continence; and still others, unmarried, were living with concubines. The synod decreed: ". . . any of the servants of God or the maids of Christ falling into carnal sin shall do penance in prison on bread and water. If it be an ordained priest, he shall be imprisoned for two years, first flogged to bleeding and afterward further disciplined at the bishop's discretion."[35]

In 952, at the Council of Augsburg, the German bishops decreed that subdeacons, deacons, priests, and bishops could not live with their wives, and that women suspected of being the concubines of the clergy were to be marked with stripes and to have their heads shaved.[36]

In 967, at the Council of Ravenna, Pope John XIII ordered married clergy to give up immediately either their wives or their ministry.[37] While trying to enforce this ruling, Ratherius of Verona promptly imprisoned and fined those members of the clergy who refused to separate from their wives.[38]

In 1022, while presiding over the Synod of Pavia, Emperor Henry II accepted Pope Benedict's VIII's series of canons ruling the deposition of all clergy who kept wives or concubines with them, and that the children of clergy who had been serfs be themselves serfs of the Church.[39]

In 1031, the Council of Bourges, attempting to eliminate clerical marriage, ruled that no one should give his daughter in marriage to a priest or a priest's son, and that no one should accept to marry the daughter of the wife of a priest. It further ruled that sons born of clergy during their ministry could not be ordained on grounds that they were illegitimate.[40]

In 1049, Libentius of Bremen forced the wives of clergy to leave the city, and had them sent, under guard, to outlying villages.[41] In that same year, Pope Leo IX anathematized married clergy, condemning them to eternal damnation.[42]

In 1051, Pope Leo IX and his Council of Rome[43] ordered the wives and concubines of priests in Rome to be seized and made slaves in the Lateran palace.[44] And he recommended to prelates throughout Christendom that they do the same, applying the policy to their own dioceses, and to seize such women for the benefit of their churches.

Around 1065, after several years of civil strife in Milan between the party upholding clerical marriage (Nicolitans) and the party condemning it (Paterins), Pope Alexander II authorized Erlembaldo to use force of arms against the Nicolitans. Archbishop Guido of Milan, supporting his married clergy, was excommunicated, attacked, and nearly beaten to death. During the riots and civil war that followed, married clergy were removed from the altar, their houses sacked, and their persons and families violated.[45]

In 1074, Pope Gregory VII decreed that no one could be admitted to orders unless he had first made a vow of celibacy. He further ruled that the laity was forbidden to attend the services of priests, deacons, or subdeacons who were not practicing continence.[46] When Gregory's rulings pertaining to continence and celibacy were read in the synods of Germany, many of the clergy there protested vehemently that the pope

> . . . was clearly a heretic and of unsound mind, who by violent interference would force men to live in the manner of angels, and while denying the ordinary course of nature, would release the restraints of fornication and filthy behavior; that if he should proceed to confirm the decision, they would choose rather to desert their priesthood than their marriages. . . .[47]

To the unutterable horror of those strict churchmen who regarded the immunity from all temporal supervision or jurisdiction as one of the most precious of ecclesiastical privileges, he [Gregory] took, as early as 1074, the decided and unprecedented step of authorizing the laity to withdraw their obedience from all prelates and priests who disregarded the canons of the Holy See on the subjects of simony and incontinence.[48]

In 1075, Pope Gregory wrote to Bertolf, Duke of Carinthia, and to Rodolf, Duke of Swabia, directing them with apostolic authority: ". . . whatever the bishops may say or not say concerning this, do you in no manner receive the ministrations of those who owe promotion or ordination to simony, or whom you know to be guilty of concubinage . . . and, as far as you can, do you prevent, by force if necessary, all such persons from officiating. And if any shall presume to prate and say that it is not your business, tell them to come to us and dispute about the obedience which we thus enjoin upon you. . . . ."[49]

In 1076, during a Roman synod, Pope Gregory suspended four French bishops and excommunicated the archbishop of Mainz for allowing married clergy.[50] Archbishop Siegfrid of Mainz had attempted, in 1074 and 1075, to impose the Gregorian rulings in his own diocese, but his own clergy rebelled against him and threatened to kill him.[51]

In Italy, as well as in France and Germany, many clergy continued to object violently to Gregory VII's attack on married priests. The Italian cities of Florence, Turin, Piacenza, and Lodi were thrown into a state of confusion and turmoil. In 1076, schismatic bishops from northern Italy gathered at Pavia and condemned Pope Gregory VII, citing, among other charges, that he had no regard for marriage and that he forced clerics to live in sin by separating them from their wives.[52] All the bishops who claimed that Gregory had no right to the papacy were excommunicated by him.[53]

Though Pope Gregory VII's unsparing and relentless efforts to assure a continent clergy were the most far-reaching and effective to date, his efforts, if contemporary descriptions are to be believed, left in his wake a married clergy, some of whom were reduced to poverty and homelessness; others mutilated and publicly paraded through the streets; still others submitted to torture, imprisonment, and lingering death—and many of the wives of clergy mocked, abused, and shamed, some of them driven to madness, others found dead in their beds or suicides.[54]

In 1099, Archbishop Manasses of Rheims ordered that married clergy who had already been deprived of office and had been excommunicated must still give up their wives. When they refused to do so, he gave orders to Robert, Duke of Flanders, that the wives be seized.[55]

In the councils of 1102 and 1108 in London, Archbishop Anselm ruled that married priests who refused to give up their wives while continuing to say Mass were to lose all legal privileges: they would be excommunicated, their personal property confiscated, and their wives made slaves of the Church.[56] And in 1107, at the Synod of Troyes, Pope Paschal II condemned married priests to deprivation and degradation.[57]

In 1123, during a general council convened by Pope Calixtus II, a canon was promulgated which not only prohibited matrimony to the clergy, but ordered that if any did marry, their marriages were to be broken and the parties subjected to penance.[58]

In 1135, at the Council of Pisa, Pope Innocent II decreed that if any clergy (subdeacons, deacons, priests, bishops, monks, or canons regular) were to marry, their marriages must be broken because "copulation of this kind, which was contracted against ecclesiastical rule, is not matrimony."[59] This ruling, reaffirmed in 1139 during Lateran II, established juridically a radical incompatibility between priesthood and marriage.

Married clergy, whose bonds of marriage might have been deemed illicit and inconsonant with clerical life, were now ruled not only illicit but invalid. Ordination would now invalidate marriage; clerical marriage itself would be regarded as concubinage, or worse; and children born of such unions would be considered illegitimate.[60] This canonical ruling, which implied a primacy of sacred orders over matrimony and defined sacred orders as nullifying present or future marriages, forced married clergy into the frightening dilemma of abandoning their wives and children, or exposing them to concubinage, illegitimacy, excommunication, poverty, slavery, or death.[61]

Although the various canons and decretals enacted between the fourth and the twelfth centuries achieved a kind of juridical plateau in the Lateran II ruling, the threats for noncompliance increased in severity; and even though many clergy, married and unmarried, decided to live continently, the fact is that from Lateran II to the late twentieth century, there has never been a time when the imposition of continence and/or celibacy has not been disputed, disregarded, or rejected by substantial numbers of the clergy. Facts demonstrating this will be presented briefly now.

THE CLERGY'S RESISTANCE TO IMPOSED CELIBACY

In 1197, at the Synod of Lanciski in Poland, clergy living in marriage or concubinage were ordered to dismiss their wives or concubines. In 1207, Pope Innocent III issued a sharp rebuke to the bishops of the province of Gnesen because married men were publicly admitted to sacred orders, and married priests continued to live with their wives and to beget children.[62]

Pope Innocent III commanded the bishops of England to address the continuing infractions of priests marrying and retaining their benefices. Councils were held, canons were passed, bishops issued pastorals. As a result, investigations were conducted, the households of priests were inspected; and those found guilty were deposed, their property assumed by the bishops, their wives excommunicated, forbidden Christian burial, and, if marital relations continued, handed over to secular authority for severe punishment.[63]

In Sweden in 1204, the archbishop of Lunden informed Innocent III that many of his clergy, in spite of repeated efforts, persisted in staying with their wives, and living in fidelity and conjugal affection with them. Innocent replied that these were to be coerced either by suspension or by deprivation of their benefice.[64]

In 1208, Innocent's legate in France, Cardinal Guala, prohibited not only wives and concubines in the residences of clergy, but also mothers and other female relatives.[65] In 1225, at Mainz, one of the canons of the national council convened by the cardinal-legate Conrad declared void the legacies of clergy to their wives, children, or concubines; further, they ordered that clergy attempting such last wills should be unburied, and that their widows, children, or concubines attempting to claim such legacies be excommunicated.[66]

In Spain in 1244, the papal legate ordered married and concubinous clergy suspended, degraded from sacred orders, and their benefices confiscated.[67] In 1274, following earlier decrees forbidding wives or concubines to live with clergy, and impositions of monetary fines for infractions, recalcitrant clergy were threatened with deprivation, their wives and concubines excommunicated, and after death, given the burial of asses.[68]

In 1250, Pope Innocent IV commanded the bishop of Ossory to deprive all married clergy of their benefices, and to remove the priestly sons of married clergy from their fathers' parishes.[69]

In 1284, prompted by the papal legate Gerard of Sabina, the Council of Amalfi decreed the dismissal, within a month, of all clergy who would not separate from their wives or concubines, suspending all prelates who might refuse to enforce this, and imposed a heavy fine on all prelates who tolerated clerical incontinence as long as the offenders would pay them a fine.[70]

In 1335, the Council of Salamanca decreed excommunicated all those providing for or attending the burial of a priest's concubine, and would not absolve them until they paid a fine to the cathedral church of fifty maravedis.[71] In 1429, the Council of Tortosa decreed imprisonment for all clergy living with concubines or wives.[72] In 1473, the Council of Aranda decreed degradation, fines, loss of benefice, and imprisonment.[73] During the same period King Ferdinand and Queen Isabella promulgated edicts subjecting clergy's wives or concubines to fines, scourging, and banishment.[74] In 1512, the Council of Seville imposed a fine of 2,000 maravedis on clergy who officiated at their children's weddings.[75]

From 1410 to 1417, William, Bishop of Paderborn, attacked with his episcopal troops the monasteries who refused to forfeit their concubines.[76]

In 1524, at the Assembly of Ratisbon in Germany, the cardinal-legate Campeggio granted permission to reactionary princes to seize and hand over to ecclesiastical authorities all married priests and monks. The church officials were empowered to imprison the offenders for life, or to turn them over to the secular powers, which frequently meant that the arrested priest or monk would be tortured to death.[77]

On September 15, 1525, Jan de Backer of Woerden, a married priest preaching against St. Peter's indulgence, was ordered by the inquisitors of Louvain to abandon his wife and to recant his errors regarding papal authority. He refused and was burned alive.[78]

From the period of the Council of Trent (1546) through the next one hundred years, the Spanish Inquisition began to treat as heretics all those who claimed that the married state was better or happier than the state of virginity or celibacy.[79]

In 1625, the Synod of Osnabruck claimed that the intransigence of the heretics was the fault of married and concubinous clergy, who provided for their children from the patrimony of the Church.[80] In 1631, the Synod of Cambray proposed waiving clerical immunity from secular powers, and asked that the secular arm be enlisted in arresting the wives and concubines of the clergy.[81]

In 1665, the Sorbonne condemned the thesis that a professed religious who thought he had a dispensation from God might licitly marry.[82]

In 1758, Desforges, a canon who had been forced into sacred orders by his family, wrote a two-volume work asserting that it was more pleasing to God that bishops and priests marry. The French Parliament had his work burned, and Desforges was imprisoned in the Bastille.[83]

In 1795, when the Reign of Terror in France had passed, some bishops assembled in Paris issued an encyclical repudiating priests who had given in to the pressures of the Revolution and married— such priests, even if they renounced their wives, were never to be absolved of their unpardonable sin.[84]

Popes Benedict XIV (1744), Pius VI (1791), and Pius VII (1808) pronounced invalid all marriages to Catholics contracted in the presence of a civil magistrate, and not (also) in the presence of a clergyman.[85] To this day, any such marriages attempted by Catholic lay persons are considered invalid;[86] such marriages attempted by clergy, whether witnessed by civil authorities or priests, are not only invalid, but incur immediate suspension from the priestly state, with the probability of degradation from the priesthood.[87]

ARE THE CANONS MANDATING CONTINENCE FOR MARRIED CLERGY AND CELIBACY FOR UNMARRIED PRIESTS WRONG?

Canons are officially promulgated ecclesial laws, whose purpose is the achievement of right order in ecclesial society.[88] Ecclesial laws have their first source and heritage in the law of the Old and New Testaments.[89] As such, canons are intended to nurture, protect, and enhance the common good of the "people of God"[90] in harmony with the will of God as revealed in the Bible.

In the Christian tradition, and indeed in the traditions of all world religions, an immoral act is understood as an offense against "God"[91] and/or created beings (including parents, family, neighbor, self, animals, neighbor's property, or the elements). In the Judeo-Christian tradition, the notion of covenant[92] as revealed in the Bible, and specifically the Ten Commandments[93] as well as the Great Commandments,[94] are the foundations on which human acts are judged moral or immoral.

Canons Mandating Continence for Married Clergy

Though it is correct to say that there were some clerical couples who, prior to and after the promulgation of the continence canons, had freely chosen to abstain from conjugal relations, there were many others who did not want to give up their marital rights or their desire for children. For this latter group, canonically required continence was a direct violation of the marriage bond. This is proven by the canons themselves, the penalties prescribed, and by the fact that large numbers of the clergy, including many bishops and even some popes, either actively resisted such canons, ignored them, or broke them.

Are Such Canons Mandating Continence for Married Clergy a Violation of God's Will as Revealed in the Ninth Commandment?

The Ninth Commandment states: "You shall not covet your neighbor's wife, you shall not set your heart on his house, his field . . . or anything that is his."[95] This commandment forbids inordinate desire or deed violating a neighbor's spouse, household, property, or belongings. It is obvious that the natural order of family and community (be it tribe, religion, village, city, or country) is radically threatened by lust, greed, envy, avarice, or any other disordered desire directed toward a neighbor's spouse or possessions. This commandment proclaims the God-given right of a family or household to live in peace, without intrusion from neighbors' disruptive attractions and deeds. It commands respect for a neighbor's spouse and home not only in action, but in the deepest recesses of one's heart and desires. Living this commandment protects the very root of society, spouses and home, from destructive interference. Civilizations throughout history bear sad witness to the moral anarchy resulting from disregarding the divine wisdom of this commandment.

Canons permanently forbidding conjugal relations are a direct violation of the Ninth Commandment. Such canons totally frustrate the twofold purpose of marriage—love and procreation. Prohibiting conjugal relations radically threatens the marriage bond itself by denying the loving expression of the very act which makes the spouses "one flesh." More will be said about this later, but the specific purpose here is to show that ecclesial laws (even those claiming to be for the good of the Church and her ministers) that violate the Commandments, God's will, and loving spouses are, in fact, destructive to the Church. The implication of such laws is that they can contradict God's law and still be valid. Church laws—or more accurately, laws promulgated by certain Church authorities who claim to be speaking for the Church or for God—that contradict or violate God's law are not valid.

Further implied by the passage of such canons regarding total abstention from spousal intercourse, is the notion that certain church authorities or synods or councils have the authority to permit or prohibit the very act of conjugal intercourse. Acceptance of this implication would bring and has, in fact, historically wrought, havoc on marital relationships. This would mean that Church authorities have power over the most vital and intimate choices between husband and wife regarding love-making and bearing children. This would lead to the dangerous conclusion that husbands and wives were bonded more to the will of Church authorities than to the will of their spouses or their own wills, even when the particular act certain Church authorities were demanding was something in violation of God's law and their marriage.

The Ninth Commandment, wholly consonant with human nature, protects marital relations and household harmony by forbidding inordinate intrusion. Canons mandating continence for married couples break this Commandment and the inviolability of the marriage union, and are, therefore, wrong.

Do Canons Mandating Continence for Married Clergy (or, for That Matter, Any Married Couple) Contradict Christ's Command?

Jesus said: "Have you not read that the Creator from the beginning made them male and female and that he said: This is why a man must leave father and mother, and cling to his wife, and the two become one body? They are no longer two, therefore, but one body. So then, what God has united, man must not divide."[96] Jesus recognizes in spousal love the creative and unifying action of God: God creating man and woman, unifying them into one body through the natural, loving bonding of intercourse and creating, by that very union, yet another image of God. Conjugal love continues the creative and unifying action of God, and no human action, save that of "scandal," is to divorce this love and this image of God. Thus, to interfere with the inviolability and indissolubility of conjugal love is to interfere with God's unitive love. To interrupt or divorce conjugal love is to violate love, human and divine.

For Jesus, who sees Abba as Father of all,[97] as holy, as completely involved with the most basic and most profound needs of his children,[98] love is the initial, abiding, and final manifestation of God. No human act more fully reveals God than love. And no divine act more fully reveals God than love. Thus, the Divine Will is that GOD, Male and Female, should intercourse through love. Love is the supreme act which is the final measure of all being, all human wisdom, all desire, and all law. And even though Jesus made the above statement in the particular context of a question about the permissibility of divorce, the truth he asserts applies in principle to an abstinence or a separation imposed by law on married clergy, as these divide husband and wife.

Canons totally forbidding conjugal relations violate God's blessing for man and woman: "Be fruitful, multiply, fill the earth. . . ."[99] Such canons stop husband and wife from becoming one body, stop them from being fruitful, from procreating, from experiencing the love, desire, and companionship revealed in man's joyful and intimate exclamation: "This at last is bone from my bones, and flesh from my flesh!"

Such canons, invoking the purity of Christ's body and the holiness of rituals and ministers, would force clergy to abstain from sexual intercourse with their wives, as if conjugal love were not a love created, given, and willed by God—as though such love were not sacred and did not reveal the very nature of God, image God as God is. Purporting to safeguard the purity of Christ's body through the altar service of pure priests,[100] they would call conjugal relations impure, a defilement,[101] thus insulting the creative act of God, the beauty and goodness of human love, and the very nature of both God and wo/man, that his love reveals.

The continence canons support the notion that the intimate desire of man for woman is not good, and is somehow a tainting and a distraction from the pure and total service of Christ and the Church. Such canons divide not only priest and wife; they divide priest and procreative love, ministerial from conjugal love, and oppose Eucharistic communion and marital union. They oppose the sacrament of the Eucharist to the sacrament of conjugal love, implying that experience of the latter precludes reception of the former. They oppose God-created conjugal relations to the good in God's Son, as though God's goodness and love and image in the very act of spousal love were incompatible with God's goodness, love, and image in Jesus.

It is one thing to distinguish between various manifestations of God's goodness and love; it is a far different thing indeed to oppose these manifestations, as though God's love contradicts and opposes itself. Yet that is precisely what canons forbidding conjugal relations imply. Such implications, and such opposition, are a theological absurdity, and a very destructive one, as the long strife-ridden history of imposed clerical continence outlined above demonstrates.

God's love at the altar does not oppose human love in the marriage bed. To pit them one against the other, to denigrate or minimize conjugal love, to say that the beauty of marital intercourse is as darkness compared to the dignity of God[102]—this is to insult God the Creator, to insult God creating in the spousal love of woman and man the very image of divinity. Thus, the continence canons break the inviolability of the marriage bond, vitiate the unitive love of God, and contradict the explicit command of Christ; they are, therefore, wrong.

Canons Mandating Celibacy as a Condition of the Priesthood

In my discussions of the ethical nature of mandated celibacy with other priests, I have heard the following objections raised: "Though I grant you that the Church may have been wrong in imposing continence on married priests, that's over with now. Today, priests freely choose celibacy. Any priest who marries is unfaithful to his vow." The case of Fr. Ivo Schmitt mentioned earlier proves that continence is still being required of married priests. To counter the statement that priests now *freely* choose celibacy, we may adduce the following data:

- The principal reason why young men do not enter the seminary is the celibacy requirement.

- Rectors of seminaries the world over will admit that many seminarians promise celibacy, not as a spontaneous and full-hearted choice, but only because it is required for the priesthood.

- The majority of Catholic priests want celibacy to be optional, as surveys over the last twenty-five years have proven again and again.

- Over 90 percent of the priests who have "resigned" the priest-hood are now married; many of them would prefer to continue their ministry, but canon law forbids them.

Further, canons 219[103] and 1026[104] defend the right of free choice regarding priesthood and choosing a state of life. Just as it would be wrong to coerce a person's choice to be a priest, so would it be wrong to coerce a person's choice to marry. Just as it would be wrong for the Church to enact laws that would require a person to become a priest or that would require priests to marry, so is it wrong to enforce laws requiring priests to be celibate. For a person who wants to be a priest, but not celibate, and who accepts celibacy only because it is canonically required for the priesthood, the celibacy canons are coercive and, therefore, wrong.

Also, the purpose of law, whether civil or ecclesial, is to promote the common good. Civil law extends to the common good of civil society; canon law, the common good of ecclesial society. The validity and morality of a particular civil law is measured in terms of that law's harmony with human nature; canon law is measured in terms of that law's harmony with nature, human and divine. The fact that people obey a law does not cause that law to be either valid or moral. Laws that violate nature, human or divine, are not only invalid but immoral. Church laws are not absolutes in themselves, nor do they become valid merely because some or many people observe them. Church laws are validated precisely in their consonance with nature, human and divine. If a particular Church law violates God's Commandment and the explicit will of Christ, a priest is obligated not to be "faithful" to it. (This does not, however, mean that a priest is allowed to have affairs, or to publicly and simultaneously have vows of celibacy and marriage. Such conduct harms women, the integrity of the priest, and the Church.)

In addition, the right to marry and to found a family is a God-given, inalienable human right.[105] This right belongs solely to individuals; it cannot be surrendered or transferred to any institution (whether civil or ecclesial), and no institution has the authority to coerce an individual's decision regarding marriage. Since God created this right, it wholly accords with God's own nature—God, who is wisdom,[106] life,[107] and generative love.[108] Man and woman, being created by God in God's image,[109] are intended for wisdom, procreative love, and life.

To interfere or coerce a person's decision regarding marriage is, therefore, to interfere with nature, human and divine. So vital to society is the free exercise of this right that its preemption or abolition might well lead society into chaos and, ultimately, extinction.

Finally, man and woman are united to each other, to Christ, and to Abba through love, whether that love be conjugal or celibate. "Beloved, let us love one another, for love is of God and he who loves is born of God and knows God. . . . God is love." Canons that forbid either conjugal or celibate love vitiate the unitive love of God.

SUMMARY

Although continence and celibacy lived with freedom and love have been a profound witness throughout Christian history, the canons mandating continence for married clergy shattered the inviolability of the marriage bond; broke the Ninth Commandment and the explicit command of Christ; and occasioned 1,700 years of heartache, strife, separation, divorce, persecution, imprisonment, despair, suicide, civil riot, and murder.

 And the canons that mandate celibacy for priests coerce human freedom; preempt the inalienable, God-given right to marry; violate nature, both human and divine; and vitiate that unitive love through which man and woman draw intimately closer to one another and to God.

All of creation is born from the love of God, and finds its joy, ecstasy, and completion in living according to the nature God gave us—to live freely, to know wisely, and to love creatively.

Thus, while praising a celibate priesthood freely and lovingly lived, we must state unequivocally that mandating continence for married priests, or celibacy for unmarried priests, is wrong.

NOTES

1. 1 Cor. 7:25–36.

2. Those Christians who died for their faith were held in great esteem by the early Church. The "Acts of the Martyrs" (written accounts detailing the trials or deaths of the Christian martyrs) were so highly regarded that St. Augustine had to warn his listeners not to put them on a level with canonical scriptures (*De anima et eius origine* 1, 10, 12). The ascetical life, complete control of the passions, and virginity came to be regarded by some early Christians as a living sacrifice, a bloodless martyrdom, an offering most pleasing to God. Cf. chapters 90–100 of the *Capita centum de perfectione spirituali* of Diadochus of Photice, PG 65, 1167–1212. See also Methodius, *On Virginity,* 7, 3 (PG 9, 641). For general reference on Christian martyrs, cf. *Acta Sanctorum,* ed. by the Bollandists (Antwerp and Brussels), 1643ff.

3. *The Paradise of the Fathers,* volumes 1 and 2 (London: Chatto and Windus, 1970; reprint Seattle, Wash.: St. Nectarios Press, 1978); *Life of St. Anthony,* H. Ellershaw trans., in *A Select Library of Nicene and Post-Nicene Fathers of the Christian Church,* Schaff and Wace, eds. (Buffalo and New York, 1886–1900; reprint Grand Rapids, Minn., 1952ff., 2d series 4 [1892], pp. 195–221); D. J. Chitty, *A Note on the Chronology of the Pachomian Foundations;* and *Patrologia syriaca,* R. Graffin and F. Nau, eds. (Berlin, 1957), pp. 379–85.

4. Celibacy in the context of this book has this general meaning: choosing an unmarried state of life for religious, ministerial, or priestly reasons. For an interesting overview of this subject of continence/celibacy and the priesthood, see Joseph Coppens, ed., *Sacerdoce et célibat* (Gembloux-Louvain, 1971); R. Gryson, *Les origines du célibat ecclésiastique du premier au septième siècle* (Gembloux: J. Duculot, 1970); E. Griffe, "Le Concile d' Elvire et les origines du célibat ecclésiastique," *Bulletin de Littérature Ecclésiastique* 4 (1973): 142–45, and 7 (1976): 123–27; Daniel Callam, "Clerical Continence in the Fourth Century: Three Papal Decretals," *Theological Studies* 41, no. 1 (1980): 3–50; Christian Cochini, *Les Origines apostoliques du célibat sacerdotal* (Paris: Lethielleux, 1981); and Karl Rahner, "Celibacy," in the *Encyclopedia of Theology,* K. Rahner, ed. (New York: Crossroad, 1975), pp. 178–84.

5. Continence in the context of this book has this general meaning: choosing to abstain from sexual intercourse for religious, ministerial,

or priestly reasons. The impetus for continence and celibacy grew out of an increasing sense of the virtues of chastity and virginity. See St. John Chrysostom, *De virginitate,* PG 48, 533–96; Gregory of Nyssa, *De virginitate;* cf. W. Moore's English translation in *A Select Library of Nicene and Post-Nicene Fathers of the Christian Church,* series 2, vol. 5, pp. 343–71; St. Thomas Aquinas, *Summa Theologica* 2–2.152.2, 2–2.152.4; Tertullian, *De exhortatione castitatis* II, 2, 7, 1; 8, 3; 13, 4; *De monogamia* 8. 4–7; *Ad uxorem,* I, 7. 4. Cf. Hippolytus, *Kata pason haireseon* 9, 12, 22; and Origen, *Homilias peri Leutikou* 4. 6.; *Kata Kelsou* 7. 48; *Tomos peri Matthaiou* 17, 35; and *Homiliai peri Louka* 17.

Proponents of clerical continence/celibacy have sometimes cited Exodus 19:15, Leviticus 15, I Samuel 21:5, or 2 Samuel 11:11 as Old Testament prototypes of a much greater purity demanded of a priest celebrating the Eucharist. Such "reasoning" obscures two far more important cultural facts concerning Judaism and its priests: marriage was considered good; barrenness a disgrace.

6. Regarding canon 33 of the Synod of Elvira: several scholars suggest this is the first known canonical legislation imposing continence on married clergy. See S. Laeuchli, *Power and Sexuality: The Emergence of Canon Law at the Synod of Elvira* (Philadelphia: Temple University Press, 1972). Edward Schillebeeckx maintains that canon 33 does not date from ca. 305 but much later, under Pope Siricius, at the end of the fourth century. E. Schillebeeckx, *The Church with a Human Face* (New York: Crossroad, 1985), pp. 240–49.

Pope Siricius justified imposing continence on married clergy by citing St. Paul's advice to married couples to abstain from sexual intercourse, "for an agreed time, to leave yourselves free for prayer" (I Cor.7:5). Siricius, relying on Jerome's argument that absolute continence is superior to marriage (PL 23, 247), further argues that marital intercourse is contaminated by "carnal concupiscence," and that if the laity are willing to sometimes abstain for prayer, how much more should bishops and priests, who are always to be ready for ministry, be always continent. Cf. Callam, *Clerical Continence in the Fourth Century,* pp. 45–46.

7. I. Cor. 7:32–35.

8. I. Cor. 7:3–6.

9. I. Cor. 7:25–31. In his *De exhortatione castitatis,* Tertullian urges his widowed friend not to remarry, stating that second marriages are contrary to God's will and opposed by St. Paul (I Cor. 7:27–28). Tertullian

grants that God tolerates such marriages, but that they are really nothing more than a kind of fornication. In *De monogamia,* written around A.D. 217 (some seven years after *De exhortatione castitatis*), Tertullian, now a Montanist, judges second marriages illicit and the next thing to adultery (see ch. 15). In *Ad uxorem,* composed between A.D. 200–206, Tertullian admonishes his wife to remain a widow after he dies. (For more on the above three treatises, see W. Le Saint, "Treatises on Marriage and Remarriage," in *Ancient Christian Writers,* J. Quasten and J. Plumpe, eds. (Westminster, Md.: Newman Press, 1951), 13:10–64.

Clement of Alexandria (*Stromata* 3, 12, 82) opposed second marriages on the grounds that matrimony was a state so sacred that even death did not completely dissolve this union (cf. also *Stromata* 3, 12, 84). John Chrysostom, in his tract *De non iterando coniugio,* advises widows not to remarry. This notion is also stated in his treatise *Ad viduam iuniorem* (PG 48, 399–410). Athenagoras of Athens was convinced that marriage was indissoluble, even after death, and termed the marriage of widows (-ers) a "decent adultery." Cf. *Apology* 33, vol. 2 of *Ante-Nicene Fathers,* J. Quasten, ed. (Westminster, Md.: Newman Press, 1953), pp. 146ff.

Christian Cochini has defended the thesis that the practice of priestly celibacy originated with the apostles in *Origines apostoliques du célibat sacerdotal;* H. Deen, repeating the thesis of Bickell (1878), also supports this interpretation (cf. *Le célibat des prêtres dans les premiers siècles de l' Église* [Paris, 1969]. But this thesis was refuted convincingly by Franz Xavier Funk in "Zölibat und Priesterehe im christlichen Altertum," *Kirchengeschichtliche Abhandlungen und Untersuchungen* 1 (Paderborn, 1897): 121–55.

10. F. Bouche-Leclerq, "Les lois démographiques d'Auguste," *Revue Historique* 57 (1895): 241–92.

11. Acts 2:14–36.

12. V. Bullough and J. Brundage, *Sexual Practices and the Medieval Church* (Buffalo, N.Y.: Prometheus Books, 1982), pp. 4–7.

13. Clement, *Stromata* III, cap. 3 (12) in NPNF, vol. 2, series 1.

14. Tertullian, *Against Marcion,* IV, cap. vii, in NPNF, vol. 2, ibid., series 1.

15. Ibid., IV, cap. xxiv.

16. Clement, *Stromata* III, cap. 17 (102).

17. Justin Martyr, *Dialogue with Trypho,* 100, NPNF series 1; also,

Erwin R. Goodenough, *The Theology of Justin Martyr* (reprint Amsterdam: Philo Press, 1923), pp. 181–82, 235–39.

18. Justin Martyr, *Apology* I, xxix, in NPNF, vol. 1, series 1.

19. Clement, *Stromata* III, cap. 12 (81).

20. Tertullian, *On Monogamy*, cap. 3, in *The Ante-Nicene Fathers*, vol. 4.

21. Bullough and Brundage, *Sexual Practices and the Medieval Church*, pp. 9–10.

22. St. Augustine, *Confessions* VIII, vii, William Watts, ed. and trans. (London: William Heinemann, 1919).

23. Derrick Bailey, *Sexual Relation in Christian Thought* (New York: Harper & Brothers, 1959), p. 54.

24. St. Augustine, *Concerning the Nature of Good*, cap. xvii, Whitney J. Oates, ed., A. H. Newman, trans., in *Basic Writings of St. Augustine*, (New York: Random House, 1948), p. 455.

25. St. Augustine, *De peccatorum meritis et remissione*, cap. 57 (XXIX), Marcus Dodd, trans., in vol. 4 of *The Works of St. Augustine*.

26. St. Gregory of Nyssa, *On Virginity*, Virginia Woods Callahan, trans., in vol. 57 of the *Fathers of the Church* (Washington, D.C.: The Catholic University of America, 1948).

27. *History of Asceticism in the Syrian Orient* (Louvain: Corpus Scriptorum Christianorum Orientalium, 1958), I: 69.

28. St. Ambrose, *De viduis*, cap. XV, lxxxviii, and cap. XI, lxix, in *Omnia Opera*, D. A. B. Caillau, ed. (Paris: Paul Mellier, 1844).

29. Origen recommended renunciation of marriage and perpetual mortification of the flesh in order to obtain complete freedom from the passions. He encouraged the celibate life and the vow of chastity for those who wanted to be true imitators of Christ: "And if we offer to Him our chastity, that is, our body's chastity, we receive from Him chastity of the spirit. . . . This is the vow of the Nazarene, which is above every other vow. For when we offer a son or a daughter, or cattle or an estate, all this is exterior to us. To offer oneself to God and to please Him, not by the labor of another, but by one's own labor, this is the most perfect and eminent of all vows; and he who does this is an imitator of Christ" (*In Num. hom.* 24, 2).

30. R. Walzer, *Galen on Jews and Christians* (London: Oxford University Press, 1949), p. 65.

31. Sozomen, *Ecclesiastical History* (London: Henry G. Bohn, 1855),

1: 23; and Socrates, *Ecclesiastical History* (London: Henry G. Bohn, 1855), 1: 2.

32. *Demonstratio evangelica,* W. J. Ferrar, trans., in *Eusebius, Proof of the Gospel* (London, 1920), 1: 9.

33. *De officiis ministrorum,* PL I, 50.

34. Cf. Augustine, *De haeresibus* 82; Ambrose, *Epistola de causa Bonosi* 63 10 (PL 16, 1192); and Jerome, *Adversus Jovinianum* 1, 3, 4 (PL 23, 239, 241: Vall).

35. Ep. 56, *Monumenta Germaniae historica epistolae selectae* I.101, trans. Emerton, pp. 92–93.

36. Henry C. Lea, *History of Sacerdotal Celibacy in the Christian Church* (New Hyde Park, N.Y.: University Books, 1966), p. 119.

37. Ibid., p. 120.

38. Ibid.

39. Ibid., p. 143.

40. Cf. Mansi 19. 503–506, especially canons 8: "Let the sons born of priests, deacons, or subdeacons in no way be accepted into the clerical state, either as priest, deacon, or subdeacon, for these men, and all those who are born in illegitimate unions, are called in sacred scripture the evil seed; neither before secular laws are they heirs, nor before the testimony of the clerk. And of these who are now clerics, let them not be admitted to sacred orders; but in whatever grade they now are, let them remain."

41. Anne L. Barstow, *Married Priests and the Reforming Papacy: The Eleventh-Century Debates* (New York: The Edwin Mellen Press, 1982), p. 39.

42. Adam of Bremen, *Gesta pontificum Hammaburgensis* III. 30, vol. 7 of *Monumenta Germaniae Historica Scriptorum,* pp. 346–47: "Praeterea multa ibidem sancita sunt ad utilitatem ecclesiae, prae quibus symoniaca haeresis et nefanda sacerdotum coniugia olographa synodi manu perpetuo damnata sunt."

43. MGH, 1826ff.

44. Lea, *History of Sacerdotal Celibacy in the Christian Church,* pp. 153–54.

45. Ibid., pp. 173ff.

46. Barstow, *Married Priests and the Reforming Papacy,* p. 67, nn. 42 and 49. C. Brooke, "Gregorian Reform in Action: Clerical Marriage in England, 1050–1200," *Cambridge Historical Journal* 12 (1956): 1–21.

47. Lambert of Hersfeld, *Annales,* G. Pertz, ed.

48. Lea, *History of Sacerdotal Celibacy in the Christian Church*, p. 190.

49. Ibid.

50. Barstow, *Married Priests and the Reforming Papacy*, p. 72.

51. Lea, *History of Sacerdotal Celibacy in the Christian Church*, p. 188.

52. Goldast, *Constitutiones Imperatorum Caesarum Augustorum ac Regum S. Imperii Romano-Theutonici* (Frankfurt, 1713), III: 314.

53. Barstow, *Married Priests and the Reforming Papacy*, p. 72.

54. Lea, *History of Sacerdotal Celibacy in the Christian Church*, p. 192.

55. Barstow, *Married Priests and the Reforming Papacy*, chapter 2, n. 17.

56. David Wilkins, *Concilia Magnae Britannae et Hiberniae* (London, 1737; Brussels, 1964), I: 410–11.

57. Lea, *History of Sacerdotal Celibacy in the Christian Church*, p. 200.

58. Ibid., p. 264.

59. Mansi, 21.489–90, canon 1: "We decree that copulation of this kind, which was contracted against ecclesiastical rule, is not matrimony."

60. Barstow, *Married Priests and the Reforming Papacy*, p. 104.

61. Ibid.

62. Lea, *History of Sacerdotal Celibacy in the Christian Church*, p. 206.

63. Ibid., p. 239.

64. Ibid., p. 207.

65. Ibid., p. 281.

66. Ibid., p. 286.

67. Ibid., p. 259.

68. Ibid., p. 260.

69. Ibid., p. 249.

70. Ibid., p. 288.

71. Ibid., p. 261.

72. Ibid., p. 263.

73. Ibid., p. 339

74. Ibid.

75. Ibid.

76. Ibid., p. 263.

77. Ibid., p. 359.

78. Ibid., p. 361.

79. Ibid., p. 464.

80. See John E. Lynch, "Marriage and Celibacy of the Clergy. The Discipline of the Western Church: An Historico-Canonical Synopsis," *The Jurist* 32, no. 1 (1972): 14–38; and "Critique of the Law of Celibacy in the Catholic Church from the Period of the Reform Councils," in William Bassett and Peter Huizing, eds., *Celibacy in the Church* (New York: Herder and Herder, 1972), pp. 57–75.

81. Ibid.

82. Ibid.

83. Ibid., p. 65.

84. Lea, *History of Sacerdotal Celibacy in the Christian Church,* p. 541.

85. Ibid., pp. 532–33.

86. *Code of Canon Law* (Grand Rapids, Mich.: William B. Eerdmans Publ. Co., 1983), canon 1108.1, p. 196.

87. Ibid., canons 1394.1 and 1087.

88. John Paul II, *Apostolic Constitution of January 25, 1983, The Code of Canon Law (in English Translation)* (Grand Rapids, Mich.: William B. Eerdmans Publishing Co., 1983), p. xiii.

89. Ibid.

90. See "Dogmatic Constitution on the Church," in *The Documents of Vatican II,* Walter Abott, ed. (New York: Guild Press, 1966), chapter 2.

91. The One referred to in the Bible as "Yahweh," "Abba."

92. Jer.31:33–34; Ez. 11:19–20.

93. Dt. 5:1–22.

94. Mt. 22:34–40; Mk. 12:28–31; Lk. 10:25–28.

95. Dt. 5:21.

96. Mt. 19:4–6.

97. Mt. 6:9–13; Lk. 11:2–4.

98. Lk. 12:22–32; Mt. 6:25–33.

99. Gen. 1:26–31.

100. Since Christ was born of a virgin he wished to be served by virgin hands (Barstow, *Married Priests and the Reforming Papacy,* pp. 59–60, citing Peter Damiani).

101. Jerome, *Adversus Jovinianum:* "Faced with the purity of Christ's body, all sexual union is impure." "A priest's wife is nothing but a snare

of the devil, and he who is ensnared thereby on to his end, he will be seized fast by the devil, and he also must afterwards pass into the hands of fiends and totally perish." Cf. B. Thorpe, *Ancient Laws and Institutes of England* (London, 1840), 2: 329, 337.

102. Ambrosiaster.

103. Canon 219: "All Christ's faithful have the right to immunity from any kind of coercion in choosing a state of life."

104. Canon 1026: "For a person to be ordained, he must enjoy the requisite freedom. It is absolutely wrong to compel anyone, in any way or for any reason whatsoever, to receive orders or to turn away from orders anyone who is canonically suitable."

105. Gen. 1:26–28, 2:18–24; Mt. 19:4–6; *Rerum Novarum: Acta Sanctae Sedis 23* (1890) 645; *Casti Connubii: Acta Apostolicae Sedis 22* (1930) 540; *Universal Declaration of Human Rights,* Article 16.1; Pope Pius XII's Christmas broadcast, 1942, in *Atti e Discorsi di Pio XII* (Rome, 1942), 4:320–21.

106. Jb. 12:13; Ps. 104:24, 136:5; Dn. 2:20; Ws. 9:13–18, and chapters 10 and 11.

107. Gen. 1 and 2; De. 30:19–20; Ws. 11:25–27; Ps. 8, 24:1–2, 147, 148; Jn. 1:4, 3:15, 4:14, 5:24, 26, 6:35, 8:58, 10:28, 11:25, 14:6; Rom. 6:23; and I Jn. 5:20.

108. Ps. 33:5, 36:5–7, 136; Jn. 3:16, 4:8, 16.

109. Gen. 1:26–27.

6

Women Priests

"And the angel said to her, 'Do not be afraid, Mary, for you have found favor with God. Listen! You are to conceive and bear a son, and you must name him Jesus. . . .' And Mary said, 'Behold, I am the handmaid of the Lord, let it be done to me according to your word.' "

Lk. 1:31–32, 38

"But the angel spoke and said to the women, 'There is no need for you to be afraid. I know you are looking for Jesus, who was crucified. He is not here, for he has risen, as he said he would. Come and see the place where he lay, then go quickly and tell his disciples, "He has risen from the dead and now is going before you to Galilee; it is there you will see him." Now I have told you.' Filled with awe and great joy, the women came quickly away from the tomb and ran to tell the disciples."

Mt. 28:5–8

ONLY A BAPTIZED MAN CAN VALIDLY
RECEIVE SACRED ORDINATION[1] (CANON 1024)

With this law, the Roman Catholic Church excludes all women from ordination to the priesthood and the episcopacy. This canon, and reasons supporting it, need to be examined because:

- Many women genuinely feel in their hearts that God is calling them to the priesthood.[2]

- Many women and men, though not interested in becoming priests themselves, nonetheless feel that excluding women from the priesthood because of their sex is discriminatory.[3]

- There is and will be an urgent need for more priests, and studies have shown that if women could be ordained, the number of women desiring some form of vocation would double.[4]

- Significant numbers of Catholic laity, priests, and bishops would approve of women being ordained.[5]

- Canons, particularly those affecting the ministry of the Church, should be consonant with their biblical heritage.[6]

Since neither canon 1024 nor the rest of the current Code of Canon Law explains why women may not receive sacred ordination, it will be helpful to turn to the "Declaration on the Question of Admission of Women to the Ministerial Priesthood," issued by the Vatican Congregation for the Doctrine of the Faith in 1977. This Declaration presents several reasons why "the Church, in fidelity to the example of the Lord, does not admit women to priestly ordination." Here we will examine two of the justifications the Vatican Declaration offers for excluding women from ordination: gender and apostolic mission.

GENDER

> . . . The priest, in the exercise of his ministry, does not act in his own name, *in persona propria*: he represents Christ, who acts through him. . . . The supreme expression of this representation is found in the altogether special form it assumes in the celebration of the Eucharist, which is the source and center of the Church's unity, the sacrificial meal in which the People of God are associated in the sacrifice of Christ: the priest, who alone has the power to perform it, then acts not only through the effective power conferred on him by Christ, but *in persona Christi,* taking the role of Christ, to the point of being his very image, when he pronounces the words of consecration.

> . . . The whole sacramental economy is in fact based upon natural signs, on symbols imprinted upon the human psychology: "Sacramental signs," says Saint Thomas, "represent what they signify by natural resemblance." The same natural resemblance is required for persons as for things: when Christ's role in the Eucharist is to be expressed sacramentally, there would not be this "natural resemblance" which must exist between Christ and his minister if the role of Christ were not taken by a man: in such a case it would be difficult to see in the minister the image of Christ. For Christ himself was and remains a man.

Though the above two paragraphs, taken from the 1977 Declaration, make several different points, the lines of reasoning pursued in both are these:

- The priest, when he pronounces the words of consecration, acts in the person of Christ, taking the role of Christ, to the point of being his very image.

- Sacramental signs require a natural resemblance to what they signify.

- When Christ's role in the Eucharist is to be expressed sacramentally, there would not be this natural resemblance if his minister were a woman—for Christ was and remains a man.

In short, a male priest images Christ in the Eucharistic consecration, but a female priest would not. A woman, solely by reason of her gender, cannot image Christ in that sacrament, "which is the source and center of the Church's unity." This might well give rise to the question among those who view this argument as merely a form of sex discrimination: If Christians believe that Christ is the fullest manifestation of God, how can they say that only men image Christ? Are women incapable of revealing God?

This question must be answered, as it affects the dignity of women, the credibility of the sacramental life of the Church, and the integrity of Church teaching. To answer this, the three following thematically related questions will be explored from a biblical perspective.

How Do Human Beings Image God?

According to the Genesis accounts[7] of creation, and the creation of man and woman:

- God created the world, and the world is good.[8]

- Man and woman are created by God,[9] in God's own image.[10]

- Man and woman, in their joyful conjugal love,[11] continue the creative work of God.[12]

- God created man and woman to live happily and lovingly, in harmony with each other, the world around them, and with God.

- All God asks of man and woman is that they not upset this "harmony," that they act according to their nature as images of God, who creates and loves. They must not act as though they were not created by God, they must not act independently of God's will (who asked them to refrain from seeking to experience evil as well as good, wrongly supposing that such experience would make them like gods).[13]

This Genesis perspective of creation stood in stark contrast to other Eastern cosmogonies, and to those religions that described the world as radically evil and humankind as the offspring of warring gods: Witness the following passages:

> God created man in the image of himself,
> in the image of God he created him,
> male and female he created them. (Gen. 1:27)

> . . . So, Yahweh God made man fall into a deep sleep. And while he slept He took one of the ribs and enclosed it in flesh. Yahweh God built the rib He had taken from the man into a woman, and brought her to the man. The man exclaimed:
> > "This at last is bone from my bones,
> > and flesh from my flesh!
> > This is to be called woman,
> > for this was taken from man."
> This is why a man leaves his father and mother and joins himself to his wife, and they become one body. Now, both of them were naked, the man and his wife, but they felt no shame in front of each other. (Gen. 2:21–25)

Thus, according to Genesis, both female and male image God in their very being. God's creative love, which gave birth to all of creation, is most reflectd by man and woman loving God and one another. Love and faith, therefore, are the preeminent human acts, which reveal God's nature and their own. When man or woman deny love, or deny their union with God, they are denying not only their own nature but God's. Chapter 3 in Genesis and, indeed, every book in both Testaments, reveals the devastating consequences when man or woman rejects God or love—shame, fear of God, mutual accusation, jealousy, divisiveness, confusion, murder, religious and political wars, and chaos.

According to the Bible, then, both female and male are created in the image of God, and are given the freedom to accept or to deny their nature. It is lack of faith and lack of love that diminish God's image, not gender. A woman or man who is loving and filled with faith is an image of God; a man or woman who is hateful and atheistic (or polytheistic) is not.

How Does Jesus Image God?

Jesus talked about God constantly; he spoke of him as Abba, as Father, as merciful, compassionate, loving, and just. Jesus cured the sick, fed the hungry, gave sight to the blind, healed lepers, embraced sinners, cast out demons, and raised the dead. He summed up all the Law and the Prophets in one great commandment: To love God with your whole heart, soul, mind, and strength, and to "love one another as I have loved you." Jesus prayed to God, begged him for strength during the most difficult trials of his life, and felt such a bond with him as to tell his friends: "The Father and I are one. . . . He who sees me, sees the Father." He prayed that all believers would experience the same oneness with God that he felt. To reveal God, Jesus was willing to be ousted from the synagogue, betrayed and abandoned by his friends, held up for public mockery, and nailed to a cross.

Jesus' life and death were testament to his love for God and others. He did not limit his love and his faith to men only or to women only.

How Do Christians Image Jesus?

Christians image Jesus by loving the way he did, by believing in God as he did. This "reflection" of Jesus is not determined in any way by gender, flesh, and blood; rather, it is determined by faith, by doing the will of God.

His mother and brothers, now arrived and standing outside, sent in a message asking for him. A crowd was sitting round him at the time the message was passed to him, "Your mother and brothers and sisters are outside asking for you." He replied, "Who are my mother and my brothers?" And looking round at those sitting in a circle about him, he said, "Here are my mother and my brothers.

Anyone who does the will of God, that person is my brother and sister and mother. . . ." (Mk. 3:31–35)

Christians witnessing to their faith are described constantly in the Acts of the Apostles, the Book of Revelation, and the Epistles of the New Testament. To proclaim the Gospel, followers of the Way were willing to sacrifice even their lives.

But Stephen, filled with the Holy Spirit, gazed into heaven and saw the glory of God, and Jesus standing at God's right hand. "I can see heaven thrown open," he said, "and the Son of Man standing at the right hand of God." At this all the members of the council shouted out and stopped their ears with their hands; then they all rushed at him, sent him out of the city, and stoned him. The witnesses put down their clothes at the feet of a young man called Saul. As they were stoning him, Stephen said in invocation, "Lord, Jesus, receive my spirit." Then he knelt down and said aloud, "Lord, do not hold this sin against them"; and with these words he fell asleep. (Acts 7:55–60)

Meanwhile Saul was still breathing threats to slaughter the Lord's disciples. He had gone to the high priest and asked for letters addressed to the synagogues in Damascus, that would authorize him to arrest and to take to Jerusalem any followers of the Way, men or women, that he could find.
  Suddenly, while he was traveling to Damascus and just before he reached the city, there came a light from heaven all round him. He fell to the ground, and then he heard a voice saying, "Saul, Saul, why are you persecuting me?" "Who are you, Lord?" he asked, and the voice answered, "I am Jesus, and you are persecuting me." (Acts 9:1–5)

Christians "image" Jesus not only by their faith, but by their love:

I give you a new commandment: love one another; just as I have loved you, you also must love one another. By this love you have for one another, everyone will know that you are my disciples. (Jn. 13:34–35)

If anyone loves me he will keep my word, and my Father will love him and we shall come to him and make our home with him. (Jn. 14:23)

As my Father has loved me, so I have loved you. Remain in my love. If you keep my commandments, you will remain in my love, just as I have kept my Father's commandments and remain in his love. I have told you this so that my joy may be in you, and your joy must be complete. (Jn. 15:9–11)

Both women and men may image Jesus. This "imaging" is not a matter of gender; it is one of faith and love. Thus, we may affirm as consistent with the entire Bible:

- Female and male are united to God through faith and love.

- Jesus is united to God through faith and love.

- Christians are united to Jesus and to Abba through faith and love.

Having established this from a biblical perspective, it is now possible to return to the Vatican Declaration's assertion that it is necessary for the priest to be male in order to image Christ. We can see how it contradicts the biblical perspective of how God is revealed, of how male and female image God, and how Christian women and men image Jesus. This assertion, pursued to its logical limits, leads to the following conclusions:

- A woman does not resemble a man.

- Thus, a woman cannot resemble Jesus.

- Therefore, a woman cannot image Jesus in the Eucharist.

But this kind of thinking, which purportedly explains why women cannot be priests, can equally spawn such disturbing syllogisms as the following:

a) Bread does not resemble a man.

Thus, bread cannot resemble Jesus.

Therefore, bread cannot image Jesus in the Eucharist.

b) A woman cannot image a man.

But Christ is a man.

Therefore, a woman cannot image Christ.

c) All men, who believe and live Jesus's law of love, image Christ.

No women, who believe and live by Jesus's law of love, image Christ.

Therefore, no women are Christian.

d) All women of faith and love (according to the Bible) image God.

No women of faith and love (according to the Vatican Declaration) image Christ.

Therefore, Christ does not image God.

Acceptance of this line of reasoning would totally undermine the Christian dignity of women, the divinity of Christ, and the Sacrament of the Eucharist, the "source and center of the Church's unity."

The Vatican has gone to extraordinary lengths to exclude women from that ministry which they think most reflects the "person of Christ"; however, it seems utter folly for them to expose themselves to accusations that they are denying the divinity of Christ, the Christianity of women, and the Eucharist in order to maintain their current policy on the ordination of women.

APOSTOLIC MISSION

According to the 1977 Vatican Declaration, "Jesus Christ did not call any woman to become part of the Twelve. . . . Jesus did not entrust the apostolic charge to women." The Declaration, in expressing "apostolic charge," cites Mark 3:14:

> . . . and he [Jesus] appointed twelve, they were to be his companions and to be sent out to preach, with power to cast out devils.

The actions of Jesus and the New Testament express in detail what power over devils means, and what message is to be preached—to proclaim that the kingdom of God is at hand;[14] that God is with us; that the kingdom of heaven is within us; and that God is Abba,[15] whose will done on earth is life, sustenance, forgiveness of sins, and deliverance from evil.[16] From this good news of God's love emanate mercy, compassion, healing, peace, wisdom, and freedom from debilitating diseases and spirits.[17] From God's love is born Jesus,[18] the anointed one,[19] the hope of the ages,[20] whose life, love, sacrifice, death, and resurrection[21] are a promise of the dignity and destiny for each one saying yes to God. This is the Good News[22] to be proclaimed, this is the "charge"[23] Jesus gave to his disciples.

But to state that Jesus gave this charge only to the Twelve, and, through them, only to their male successors is to misinterpret what Jesus did. He "sent" the Twelve,[24] he sent the seventy-two,[25] he sent those in the upper room at Pentecost,[26] he sent men and women, Jew and Gentile to proclaim the Good News and to live his commandment of loving others as he did.

In her "fiat"[27] to the will of God, Mary became pregnant, nurturing in her womb "Emmanuel."[28] Her "yes" bore into the world the body and blood that is Jesus.[29] In her Magnificat[30] Mary glorifies the wondrous deeds of God. Her cousin Elizabeth greets her: "Why should I be honored with a visit from the mother of my Lord?" Magi offer Jesus homage at his birth.[31] Anna the prophetess, when Jesus is brought to the Temple as an infant, praises God and speaks of Jesus to all who look forward to the deliverance of Jerusalem.[32]

The Gospel of John describes Mary, at the wedding feast of Cana, inviting the first sign (miracle) revealing Jesus' glory; this miracle prompted their faith in him.[33] Jesus said of a Roman centurion: ". . . not even in Israel have I found faith like this."[34] A Samaritan woman opens the way for faith to her neighbors.[35] In a crowd of people pressing in upon Jesus, a woman with a flow of blood says in the silence of her heart: "If I but touch the hem of his cloak I will be well again. . . ." and Jesus heals her, saying: "Courage, my daughter, your faith has made you well."[36] Mary of Bethany anoints Jesus, in preparation for his death.[37] While all the apostles (save John) were hiding,[38] the women stood at the foot of the cross while the man they loved most in the world suffered a hideous, shameful death.[39] Women were the first to announce to the unbelieving "apostles" that Jesus had risen from death.[40]

It is clear from the Gospels that Jesus did not establish a male hierarchy of authority; he inspired a universal proclamation of God's love, God's being in us—an abiding, ultimate Truth which gives birth to service, virtue, healing, forgiveness, respect, kindness, dignity, equality, and understanding. Instead of establishing a hierarchy of power, either spiritual or temporal, Jesus inspired a proclamation and ministry of love. Jesus did not endow the Twelve with an exclusive authority. His "apostolic charge" to them was the same that he gave to all: believe in God's presence and love,[41] repent,[42] forgive,[43] love your neighbor and God.[44]

James and John asked to sit in positions of authority when Jesus established his messianic reign:

> . . . when the other ten heard this they were indignant with the two brothers. But Jesus called them to him and said, "You know that among the pagans the rulers lord it over them and make their authority felt. This is not to happen among you. No, anyone who wants to be great among you must be your servant, and anyone who wants to be first among you must be your slave, just as the son of Man came not to be served but to serve, and to give his life as a ransom for many. (Mt. 20, 24–28)

From the passages cited above, it is clear that neither gender nor apostolic charge determine how a Christian reflects, reveals, or "images" Jesus. One does this, rather, by doing the will of God and the will of Jesus, which is one with God's. Indeed, the proclamation of Jesus and God is the same:

> Man and Woman are created by God; God, who is Love, sent the Law, the Prophets, and his Son to reveal this; man and woman, by nature, are meant to love God and each other—this is wisdom, this is life, this is union, this is the fullness of joy, this is the kingdom of Heaven.[45]

Many stories in the Bible have all too starkly demonstrated the misfortune and tragedy accompanying denials of this original truth. Excluding women from priestly ministry on the basis of gender and apostolic charge is but another in a long list of abuses resulting directly from confusing "form" and will. It is will that unites or divides; that affirms or denies, loves or hates, images or disintegrates. It is will as abiding intention or specific choice that finally determines whether God or evil, being or destruction, are imaged in the world. It is will, not gender or power, that images the Divine.

Man and woman, in the very act of loving one another and God, image God. Christian man and woman in the very act of loving one another and God, image Christ. It is love which images God and Christian love which images Christ. This love and this imaging are not the exclusive prerogative of man only—they are the birthright and fulfillment of both woman and man. Conversely, if they deny the will of God expressed in their very nature, and says no to the God in whose image they are created, disharmony, mutual accusation, and subjugation follow.[46]

This specific choice to deny God in human nature is both idolatrous and anti-human. It is idolatrous because man and woman usurp the will of God by claiming equality with him;[47] it is anti-human because this choice of denying that man and woman are, indeed, the created image of God pits male and female against one another, the world, and God.

Man and woman today are no more, no less, than they were in the beginning: the choice of yes or no to God and to God's image in human nature is there for all to make. It is not that Adam and Eve sinned once and humanity has been paying for it ever since; it is, rather, that Adam and Eve are man and woman in all times, in all places. The authors of the book of Genesis described male and female and the world as God continues to create them. Genesis presents a timeless Truth, as vital and as inspired now as when it was written. Original sin is not a form of evil endowment passed unwillingly into the souls of all human beings; it is that unique choice each person makes to affirm or deny his or her own nature in God.

Original sin is saying no to self and others as God created us; it is saying no to happiness, to wisdom, and to love—original sin is saying no to life, to the true nature of creation, to the harmony of heaven and earth, God and wo/man, male and female. From this original denial initiate error, destructive will, and a disordered life. Once unleashed in the human heart, this denial threatens self, others, nature, relationships, covenant, communion, and all that is good.

The effects of this denial of human nature and God are evident in everything from the global nuclear threat to neighborhood violence. The effects of this denial are evident in the ever-present and pervasive tension between man and woman. It is not necessary to read the remarks of Plato,[48] Aristotle,[49] and Aquinas[50] on the inferiority of women, or the slurs on women uttered by various popes[51] and papal legates;[52] it is not necessary to know of peoples and cultures who would expose or abandon till death female infants[53]—none of this knowledge is necessary to be aware that division, opposition, subjection, and competition constantly darken female-male relations.

We may now answer the question: Are canon 1024 and the 1977 Declaration on the admission of women to the priesthood consonant with their biblical heritage? And our answer is no, because they contradict both the image of God that men and women are created to be, and the image of Jesus, who is manifested in faith and love. Canon 1024 and the 1977 Declaration are, therefore, not only invalid but destructive.

NOTES

1. In November 1991, a scripture scholar from southern Europe made this comment: "According to Tertullian, sacred ordination or 'ecclesiastical ordo' was instituted by the Church, imitating the Roman 'ordines': 'ordo senatorius' and 'ordo equestris,' that is, the Church aristocracy over against the 'plebs' or common people." He went on to say that the Letter to the Hebrews shows that Christ is the high priest who has offered a perfect single offering: "There is no longer a need for more offerings, or for the priesthood" (cf. Hebrews 10:1–18; 9:15–28).

Regarding this point of view and its vast implications, further research is required. Suffice to say at this time that even if sacred ordination reflected Roman custom, and not the mind of Jesus, this would not explain away the fact that Jesus' disciples, within a very short time after his death, began gathering together for "the breaking of the bread." Nor would it explain away Jesus' words during the last supper he shared with his friends: "Take and eat, this is my body. . . . Take and drink, this is my blood, which will be shed for you. . . . Do this in memory of me."

2. See J. Coriden, *Sexism and Church Law* (New York: Paulist Press, 1977); *Women and Catholic Priesthood: An Expanded Vision, Proceedings of the Detroit Ordination Conference,* Anne Gardiner, ed. (New York: Paulist Press, 1976); and *Women and Orders*, R. Heyer, ed. (New York: Paulist Press, 1974).

3. S. Callahan, "Misunderstanding of Sexuality and Resistance to Women Priests," in *Women Priests: A Catholic Commentary,* A. and L. Swidler, eds. (New York: Paulist Press, 1977), pp. 291–94.

4. Dean R. Hoge, *Report I, Study of Future Church Leadership* (Washington, D.C.: Catholic University of America, 1986), p. 22. See also R. Fuller, "Pro and Con: The Ordination of Women in the New Testament," in M. Micks and C. Price, eds., *Toward a New Theology of Ordination* (Sommerville, Mass.: Green, Hadden & Co., 1976), pp. 1–11.

5. See chapter 4.

6. "A second question arises: What is the code? For an accurate answer to this question, it is necessary to remind ourselves of that distant heritage of law contained in the books of the Old and New Testaments. It is from this, as from its first source, that the whole juridical and legislative tradition of the Church derives." Pope John Paul II, Apostolic Constitution promulgating the 1983 Code of Canon Law, January 25, 1983.

See also L. Vasquez, "The Position of Women According to the Code," *The Jurist* 34, no. 9 (1974): 128–42.

    7. Genesis, chapters 1 and 2.

    8. Gen. 1:31.

    9. Gen. 2:26–27.

  10. Ibid.

  11. Gen. 2:23–24.

  12. Gen. 1:28–31, 2:18–25.

  13. Gen. 2:16–27, 3:4–6.

  14. Mk. 1:14–15.

  15. The One Jesus calls "Father." Cf. Mt. 6:9–13; Lk. 11:2–4. Jesus seems to bring a new revelation of the meaning of the term "covenant," which appears 289 times in the Bible, according to Nelson's *Complete Concordance of the New American Bible,* Fr. Stephen Hartdegen, general editor (New York: Thomas Nelson Inc., Publishers, 1977). This term, and indeed the entire Bible, express the relationship between God and humankind. But Jesus sees this covenant as expressing more than the bond between humankind and the creator, provider, protector, law-giver, and source of wisdom and salvation; he sees it as a very personal and intimate relationship between parent and child.

  16. Lk. 11:4; Mt. 6:13.

  17. The Gospels reveal many such actions; for example, in the Gospel of Luke: 4:31–41, 5:12–26, 6:6–11, 7:1–17, 36–50, and 8:26–56, 9:37–43, 13:10–17, 14:1–6, 17:11–19, 18:35–43.

  18. Jn. 3:16.

  19. Mt. 26:57–66; Mk. 14:53–64; Lk. 22:66–71; Jn. 10:22–39.

  20. Lk. 1:54–55.

  21. Jn. 20 and 21; Lk. 24; Mk. 16; Mt. 28.

  22. Mk. 16:16.

  23. Acts 1:7–8; Jn. 20–21, 23; Mt. 28:18–20. Of "the Twelve" as eschatological and symbolic rather than historical-masculine, see Elizabeth Schüssler Fiorenza, "The Twelve," in A. and L. Swidler, eds., *Women Priests,* pp. 114–20. See also R. Norris, Jr.'s, "The Ordination of Women and the 'Maleness' of the Christ," *Anglican Theological Review,* suppl. series, no. 6 (June 1976): 69–80.

  24. Lk. 9:1–6. See also Elizabeth Schüssler Fiorenza, "The Apostleship of Women in Early Christianity," in *Women Priests,* pp. 135–40. In addition,

see Bernadette Brooten, "Junia . . . Outstanding Among the Apostles," in *Women Priests,* pp. 141–44.

25. Lk. 10:1–20.
26. Acts 2ff.
27. Lk. 1:38.
28. Mt. 1:23–24.
29. Mt. 1:25; Lk. 2:1–20; Jn. 1:12–14.
30. Lk. 1:46–55.
31. Mt. 2:1–12.
32. Lk. 2:36–38.
33. Jn. 2:1–12.
34. Mt. 8:5–13; Lk. 7:1–10; Jn. 4:46–53.
35. Jn. 4:1–42.
36. Mt. 9:18–22; Mk. 5:21–34; Lk. 8:40–48.
37. Jn. 12:1–11; Mk. 14:3–9; Mt. 26:6–13.
38. Jn. 19:25–27, 20:19; Mk. 14:49–50, 15:40–41; Mt. 26:56, 27:55–56.
39. Mt. 27:45–54; Mk. 15:33–41; Lk. 23:44–49; Jn. 19:28–30.
40. Jn. 20:18; Lk. 24:9–11; Mk. 16:10–11; Mt. 28:8–10.
41. Mt. 10:1–33; Mk. 3:13–15, 6:7; Lk. 9:1ff.
42. Mt. 11:20–24; Lk. 10:13–15.
43. Lk. 11:4; Mt. 6:12, 18:21–35.
44. Mt. 22:34–40; Mk. 12:28–34; Lk. 10:25–37; Jn. 13:34–35.
45. Jn. 14:7, 23, 17:3; I Jn.: 1–5.
46. Gen. 3ff.
47. Gen. 3:4–6.
48. E.g., Plato, *Timaeus* 91, from the *Dialogues of Plato,* B. Jowett, trans. (London: Oxford University Press, 1931), 3: 513.
49. *The Complete Works of Aristotle,* the revised Oxford translation, J. Barnes, ed. (Princeton University Press, 1984), vols. 1 and 2, esp. 648a 12; 728a 18; 737a 28; 775a 16; 951a 12; 1254b 14; 1259a 39; 1260a 9; and 1343b 30.
50. St. Thomas Aquinas, *Summa Theologiae* Ia, 92 and 93, E. Hill, trans. (New York: McGraw-Hill, 1964), 13: 35–85. See also "Thomas Aquinas: The Man Who Should Have Known Better," in E. Clark and H. Richardson, *Women and Religion* (New York: Harper & Row, 1977), pp. 75–101.
51. Notably Siricius, Gregory the Great, Gregory VII, Calixtus II,

Alexander III, and Innocent III.

52. Especially Peter Damiani; see H. Lea, *History of Sacerdotal Celibacy*, (New Hyde Park, N.Y.: University Books, 1966), pp. 143–66. See also R. Ruether, "Misogynism and Virginal Feminism in the Fathers of the Church," in R. Ruether, ed., *Religion and Sexism* (New York: Simon and Schuster, 1974), pp. 150–83.

53. Among many instances: Sparta, especially during the Peloponnesian Wars; China, during the famine periods of the Ming Dynasty; and the Gurani Indians of South America during their enslavement period under the Spanish and the Portuguese.

7

Authority[1]

"When the other ten heard this they were indignant with the two brothers. But Jesus called them to him and said, 'You know that among the pagans the rulers lord it over them, and their great men make their authority felt. This is not to happen among you. No; anyone who wants to be great among you must be your servant, and anyone who wants to be first among you must be your slave, just as the Son of Man came not to be served but to serve, and to give his life as a ransom for many.'"

Mt. 20:24–28

"But Jesus turned and said to Peter, 'Get behind me, Satan! You are an obstacle in my path, because the way you think is not God's way but man's.'"

Mt. 16:23

Even the briefest of glances at recent geopolitical events will reveal that temporal authority is in crisis. The cries for freedom and democracy resounding in Moscow and Beijing demonstrate the turmoil resulting from a political authority that fails to meet the needs of its people. The Arab-Israeli conflict, the Vietnam War, the Iran-Iraq War, and the Persian Gulf War all prove how frequently international order is disrupted by national interests.

The disintegration of Soviet communism, and the resulting confusion concerning accountability for the former USSR's nuclear arsenal, underscores a potential for destruction far more terrifying than any of the conflicts mentioned above. How did it ever come to pass that the presidents of the two most powerful nations on earth possess the "authority" to begin a war that could destroy the planet? How many of the nearly five billion people in the world would want two men to have the power to decide their very existence?

The Roman Catholic Church is similarly suffering a crisis of authority not only within its own hierarchy regarding priestly ministry, but also among its 900,000,000 members on matters they consider vital. In the United States, this crisis of authority is revealed in a number of issues and cases. In a *Los Angeles Times* nationwide poll, published August 23, 1987, only 14 percent of respondents believed that the pope is infallible. A 1985 *New York Times*/CBS poll[2] found that 83 percent of the Catholic population between the ages of eighteen and thirty-nine favor use of artificial birth control. In the same age category, 68 percent favor women as priests; 69 percent favor letting priests marry; 80 percent favor permitting Catholics to divorce and remarry; and 86 percent think it is possible to disagree with the pope on birth control, abortion, or divorce and still be a good Catholic.

We may cite several examples of official Church suppression of all forms of heterodoxy. In 1986, Fr. Charles Curran of Catholic University in Washington, D.C., was stripped of his teaching authority as a Catholic theologian for presenting a moral perspective on sexual issues that was at variance with official Church teaching. In the same year, Archbishop Hunthausen of Seattle, stripped of five areas of authority in his diocese, appealed to the assembled National Conference of Catholic Bishops; he was officially told that the conference did not have the authority to intervene in a matter involving the Holy See and an individual bishop. Twenty-eight signers of a 1984 "Catholic Statement on Pluralism and Abortion" published in the

New York Times, were threatened with dismissal from their religious communities. Matthew Fox was formally silenced because of his writings on feminist theology and creation spirituality. Rev. John McNeil, a psychiatrist and moral theologian, was dismissed from the Jesuit Order because of his ministry to homosexuals. Sarabeth Eason, a twelve-year-old girl, was expelled from a Catholic school in Ohio because of her pro-choice views on abortion. Guidelines have been issued prohibiting female servers on the altar. Rev. Michael Buckley's appointment as theological advisor to the National Conference of Catholic Bishops was reviewed on the grounds that he signed a 1977 statement along with twenty-two other Jesuit theologians protesting the methodology and conclusions of the Vatican Declaration, "On the Admission of Women to the Ministerial Priesthood." Fr. Barry Brunsman, a Franciscan, was ordered to leave the Monterey diocese after an inquiry letter from the Vatican concerning his book *New Hope for Divorced Catholics,* which suggested more frequent use of the "internal forum" solution to divorced and remarried Catholics who want their new marriages blessed in order to return to full participation in the Sacraments. Fr. William Callahan, a Jesuit for forty years, co-director of the Quixote Center, and nationally known social justice advocate for humanitarian aid to Nicaragua and equality for women in the Catholic Church, had been ordered under threat of dismissal to "make no public statements critical of the Church or any of its leadership . . . ," and to end his involvement with the organizations Catholics Speak Out and Priests for Equality.

There are several other indicators of a growing crisis in religious authority:

- In a 1970 survey of resigned priests in the United States, the primary reason given for resignations was conflict with authority.[3]

- In the United States, with its Catholic population of some 55 million, there are approximately ten million divorced Catholics.[4] Of these, the majority have remarried; but from 1973 to 1983 only 30,000 annulments have been granted. This means that millions of U.S. Catholics, under the burden of official Church teaching prohibiting remarriage, feel forbidden to receive the Eucharist and absolution.

- Though precise national figures are difficult to determine, it is estimated that 10 percent of the population in the United States, including the Catholic population, is gay. This would mean there are some 5,500,000 Catholics whose sexual orientation conflicts with Church teaching. According to a *New York Times*/CBS poll, 51 percent of American Catholics favor legalizing homosexual relations between consenting adults.

- With official Church teaching prohibiting all "artificial" means of birth control, many priests have ordered their parishioners to give up either the Eucharist or their practice of birth control. And though it is impossible to estimate precisely how many American Catholics have been so ordered, and how many others have, in conscience, excluded themselves from the Sacraments because of this conflict, it is reasonable to say that birth control teaching has been one of the most contested and divisive issues facing the Church today. When 83 percent of American Catholics between the ages of eighteen and thirty-nine favor the use of artificial birth control, and official Church teaching condemns it, the pastoral implications of this conflict are staggering.

- Worldwide, over 100,000 priests[5] and 300,000 nuns[6] have left their communities since Vatican II. Over 40 percent of the world's parishes do not have a resident pastor.

Although Vatican II defined the Church as "the People of God," and even though many of those same people are calling for a voice in shaping the ecclesial teachings and policies that so intimately affect their lives, the fact is that during the 1988 International Synod on the Laity, not one lay person out of nearly a billion Catholics had even a single vote on any of the policies affecting the lives of the laity. This sobering fact seems quite consistent with Pope John Paul's statement during his 1987 visit to the United States, "The Church is a theocratic institution, not a democratic one."

In the 1989 Cologne Declaration, 186 European theologians publicly expressed their concern over three matters: the Curia's filling of episcopal sees without respecting the suggestions and established rights of local churches; the Vatican's refusal to grant qualified theologians official church permission to teach; and the pope's "linking the teaching on birth control with the fundamental truths of the faith like the divinity of God and salvation through Jesus Christ."[7]

In the face of this growing dissent, the papacy of John Paul II reasserts the Vatican I and II teachings on primacy[8] and infallibility[9] in matters of faith and morals solemnly defined:[10]

> The Roman pontiff, when he speaks *ex cathedra,* that is, when exercising the office of pastor and teacher of all Christians, he defines with his supreme apostolic authority a doctrine concerning faith and morals to be held by the universal Church, through the divine assistance promised to him in blessed Peter, is possessed of that infallibility with which the divine Redeemer wills his Church to be endowed in defining faith and morals: and therefore such definitions of the Roman pontiff are irreformable of themselves (and not from the consent of the Church). (DS 3074)
>
> If—which God may avert—anyone should presume to contradict this definition of ours, let him be anathema. (DS 3075)

Further, this same papacy demands assent of intellect and will[11] from the entire Church not only in matters solemnly defined, but also in matters defined by the teaching magisterium of the Church, whether assembled in formal council[12] or acting as pastor of a diocese. These "matters" include not only definitions about God, Jesus, the Holy Spirit, Incarnation, Resurrection, Mary, the seven sacraments, and papal infallibility, but also all aspects of morality, personal and social, including premarital sex, divorce and remarriage, and birth control.

Certain comparisons can be made between this kind of papal authority and the political hegemony of recent American and Soviet presidents, particularly in the stockpiling of nuclear weapons as mutual deterrents:

- Both forms of authority make absolute claims. The nuclear authority claims power to end all human life. The religious authority claims power from God to "bind and to loose" from sin, from the Church, and from eternal life.

- Both forms of authority claim final and superior knowledge over their constituencies. The presidents claim unparalleled knowledge into the delicate balance of global political and nuclear power. The pope claims infallible, irreformable truth.

- Both forms of authority claim unilateral decision-making power. In the act of defining religious truths or authorizing nuclear attack, neither presidents nor popes are obligated to the will of their constituencies.

- Both forms of authority are radically preemptive. Both presume final power over the lives, knowledge, and choices of their constituencies.

While some might find security and efficiency in this kind of authority, and appreciate it as a kind of global culmination of political and religious evolution, many others find it deeply disturbing to realize that two men have had the authority to annihilate five billion people; and that one man, with a constituency of nearly one billion, claims authority over all others to define faith, morals, and Church discipline.

How does this authority compare with the covenant God established with the House of Israel?

Deep within them I will plant my Law, writing it on their hearts. Then I will be their God and they shall be my people. There will be no further need for neighbor to try to teach neighbor, or brother to say to brother, "Learn to know Yahweh!" No, they will all know me, the least no less that the greatest. . . . (Jer. 31:33–34)

How does this authority reflect the promise of Jesus?

> You are my friends, if you do what I command you. I shall not
> call you servants anymore, because a servant does not know his master's
> business; I call you friends, because I have made known to you every-
> thing I have learnt from my Father. . . .
>   If anyone loves me, he will keep my word, and my Father will
> love him, and we shall come to him and make our home with him.
> (Jn. 16:15, 15:23)

What kind of authority is it that sets itself above others and claims
to define for all others the meaning of faith and morals? This chapter
will examine, from biblical and pastoral perspectives, the Church's
"hierarchical" and "inerrant" doctrinal authority.

ECCLESIAL AUTHORITY

To understand more fully the nature of ecclesial authority, two abiding
notions must be examined; viz., that ecclesial authority is hierarchical,
and that when solemnly exercised, it is assisted by the Holy Spirit,
and hence infallible and worthy of full obedience.

Hierarchical Authority

Vatican Councils I and II defined authority in the Church as hierarchical, originating in the authority of Christ, the supreme high priest,
who in turn delegated his authority preeminently to Peter and to
the rest of his apostles. The apostles appointed bishops, who in their
turn appointed priests and deacons to carry on their mission.[13]

> This most sacred Synod, following in the footsteps of the First Vatican
> Council, teaches and declares with that Council that Jesus Christ,
> the eternal Shepherd, established His holy Church by sending forth
> the apostles as He Himself had been sent by the Father. He willed

that their successors, namely the bishops, should be shepherds In His Church even to the consummation of the world.

In order that the episcopate itself might be one and undivided, He placed blessed Peter over the other apostles, and instituted in him a permanent and visible source and foundation of unity of faith and fellowship. And all this teaching about the institution, the perpetuity, the force and reason for the sacred primacy of the Roman pontiff and of his infallible teaching authority, this Sacred Synod again proposes to be firmly believed by all the faithful.

Continuing in the same task of clarification begun by Vatican I, this Council has decided to declare and proclaim before all men its teaching concerning bishops, the successors of the apostles, who together with the successor of Peter, the Vicar of Christ and the visible Head of the whole Church, govern the house of the living God.[14]

Another delineation of hierarchical authority is found in Vatican II documents on the relationship of bishops to the Universal Church:

By virtue of sacramental consecration and hierarchical communion with the head and other members of the college, a bishop becomes part of the episcopal body. "The order of bishops is the successor to the college of the apostles in the teaching authority and pastoral rule; or, rather, in the episcopal order the apostolic body continues without a break. Together with its head, the Roman pontiff, and never without its head, the episcopal order is the subject of supreme and full power over the universal Church. But this power can be exercised only with the consent of the Roman pontiff."[15]

According to this hierarchical structure, priests are assistants to the bishops, and receive their authority from them to minister to the faithful.

Christ, whom the Father sanctified and sent into the world has, through His apostles, made their successors, the bishops, partakers of His consecration and His mission. These in their turn have legitimately handed on to different individuals in the Church various degrees of participation in their ministry. Thus the divinely established ecclesi-astical ministry is exercised on different levels by those who from antiquity have been called bishops, priests, and deacons. Although priests do not possess the highest degree of the priesthood, and although they are dependent on the bishops in the exercise of their power, they are nevertheless united with the bishops in sacerdotal dignity. By the power of the sacrament of orders, and in the image of Christ the eternal High Priest, they are consecrated to preach the gospel, shepherd the faithful, and celebrate divine worship as true priests of the New Testament.

Defined as successor of Peter and head of the whole Church, the Roman pontiff stands at the apex of this hierarchy, and "by divine institution he enjoys supreme, full, immediate, and universal authority over the care of souls."

For our Lord made Simon Peter alone the rock and key-bearer of the Church, and appointed him shepherd of the whole flock.[16]

This hierarchical definition of authority proclaims the following:

a) The pope is the spiritual successor of Peter.

b) Peter, by divine will, possessed full, immediate, and supreme authority over the care of souls.

c) The pope is "first" among all the successors of Peter, and he is infallible.

d) Christ entrusted his mission of salvation to the apostles, and he intended them to entrust the authority of his mission to bishops.

e) The authority of Christ's mission is capable of being assigned in virtue of consecration, and capable of being measured by the degree of "holy orders" conferred.

f) Bishops, priests, deacons, and finally laity share, in descending degrees, the authority of Christ.

g) Christ intended to found a church with his authority exercised hierarchically.

Infallible Authority, Worthy of Full Obedience

The dogmatic constitution of the Church (titled *Lumen Gentium,* from the Documents of Vatican II) instructs the Catholic faithful on the obedience owed to the hierarchy, and in particular to the pope.

> In matters of faith and morals, the bishops speak in the name of Christ and the faithful are to accept their teaching with a religious assent of soul. This religious submission of will and of minds must be shown in a special way to the authentic teaching authority of the Roman pontiff, even when he is not speaking *ex cathedra.* That is, it must be shown in such a way that his supreme magisterium is acknowledged with reverence, and the judgments made by him are sincerely adhered to, according to his manifest mind and will.[17]

Vatican II declares papal infallibility to be as encompassing as the entire deposit of revelation, and irreformable—even when exercised without the consent of the Church:

> This infallibility with which the divine Redeemer willed His Church to be endowed in defining a doctrine of faith and morals extends as far as extends the deposit of divine revelation, which must be religiously guarded and faithfully expounded. This is the infallibility which the Roman pontiff, the head of the college of bishops, enjoys in virtue of his office, when, as the supreme shepherd and teacher of all the faithful, who confirms his brethren in their faith, he proclaims by a definitive act some doctrine of faith and morals. Therefore his definitions, of themselves, and not from the consent of the Church, are justly styled irreformable, for they are pronounced with the assistance of the Holy Spirit, an assistance promised to him in blessed Peter. Therefore they need no approval of others, nor do they allow an appeal to any other judgment. For then the Roman pontiff is not pronouncing judgment as a private person. Rather, as the supreme teacher of the Universal Church, as one in whom the charism of

the infallibility of the Church herself is individually present, he is expounding or defending a doctrine of the Catholic faith.[18]

The constitution says also that definitions of faith and morals originating from bishops assembled in ecumenical council must be adhered to "with the submission of faith."

This obedience of faith, intellect, and will is due the pope and bishops because they are, the constitution says, endowed with "the authority of Christ" as well as "successors of the apostles," who received from Christ, through the Holy Spirit, the mission and power to proclaim the gospel and to teach all nations.

> Just as the role that the Lord gave individually to Peter, the first among the apostles, is permanent and was meant to be transmitted to his successors, so also the apostles' office of nurturing the Church is permanent, and was meant to be exercised without interruption by the sacred order of bishops. Therefore, this Sacred Synod teaches that by divine institution bishops have succeeded to the place of the apostles as shepherds of the Church, and that he who hears them, hears Christ, while he who rejects them, rejects Christ and Him who sent Christ.[19]

The above declarations (*Lumen Gentium,* chapter 3, par. 20) regarding obedience due the pope and the bishops are constructed on the following premises:

a) The bishops and the pope, when speaking of matters of faith and morals, speak in the name of Christ.

b) When the bishops are assembled in ecumenical council, and when they solemnly define matters pertaining to faith and morals, such definitions are infallible.

c) When the pope, in virtue of his office as supreme shepherd and teacher of all the faithful, solemnly defines some doctrine regarding faith and morals, such doctrine is infallible and irreformable.

d) When the pope or the bishops assembled in formal council, solemnly define matters pertaining to faith and morals, the faithful must adhere to these definitions with the submission of their minds, their wills, their souls, and their faith.

e) Obedience to the pope and bishops in matters of faith and morals solemnly defined is obedience to Christ, and rejection of such solemn teaching is rejection of Christ and the One who sent him.

f) Christ intends his teachings regarding faith and morals to be infallible, irreformable, and adhered to with total submission of mind, will, soul, and faith.

QUESTIONS CONCERNING HIERARCHICAL AUTHORITY: A BIBLICAL PERSPECTIVE

It is consistent with the New Testament to say that Jesus, during his public ministry, selected the "Twelve"[19] and sent them forth to proclaim the reign of God and to dispel demons and sicknesses. It is also consonant with Scripture to say that Jesus, risen from the dead, appeared to eleven of these twelve men and instructed them to proclaim the Good News to all nations, to baptize in God's name, and to teach observance of the commandments. Further, it is consonant with human reason to say that any institution, including an ecclesial one, requires order. But, in light of the solemn declarations of Vatican Councils concerning hierarchical authority, the following questions should be asked:

1) Did Jesus, in selecting the Twelve and commissioning them to proclaim the Good News and to dispel demons and diseases, intend that only the Twelve, and those appointed by them as successors, would possess this authority?

2) Did Jesus appoint Peter to be the leader of the Twelve, with all the others subject to Peter's authority?

3) Did Jesus intend to establish a hierarchical authority?

Regarding Question 1

While Scripture does state that Jesus selected twelve men, and authorized them to proclaim the reign of God and to dispel demons and sicknesses, it does not assert that Jesus entrusted this authority exclusively to the Twelve, nor that Jesus told them that only those delegated by the apostles would have this power.

That this authority was not entrusted exclusively to the Twelve and their successors is demonstrated in the conversion, apostolic claim, and activity of Paul of Tarsus.[20] It is further demonstrated in the identical authority Jesus entrusted to the seventy-two disciples:

> After this the Lord appointed seventy-two others and sent them out ahead of him, in pairs, to all the towns and places he himself was to visit. He said to them, ". . . Cure those in it who are sick, and say, 'The kingdom of God is very near to you.' . . . Anyone who listens to you listens to me; anyone who rejects you rejects me, and those who reject me reject the one who sent me." (Lk. 10: 1, 2, 9, 16)

It is also demonstrated in the fact that Jesus reprimanded one of the Twelve who tried to stop an outsider from exorcising demons in Jesus's name:

> John spoke up. "Master," he said, "we saw a man casting out devils in your name, and because he is not with us we tried to stop him." But Jesus said to him, "You must not stop him: anyone who is not against you is for you." (Lk. 9:49, 50)

This is also demonstrated in numerous instances of persons other than the Twelve and their appointees proclaiming the Kingdom of God. These persons include, among others, Mary[21] (the mother of Jesus), Elizabeth,[22] Simeon,[23] Anna,[24] John the Baptist,[25] the Samaritan woman at the well,[26] the demoniac of Gerasa,[27] Mary of Bethany,[28] the man born blind,[29] the thankful leper who had been cured by Jesus,[30] the Canaanite woman,[31] the centurion whose servant was sick,[32] Mary of Magdala,[33] and the other women at the tomb of Jesus.

Regarding Question 2

Scripture records this saying of Jesus to Peter, after the latter had identified Jesus as the Messiah and son of the living God:

> Simon, son of Jonah, you are a happy man! Because it was not flesh and blood that revealed this to you but my Father in heaven. So I now say to you: You are a stone and on this rock I will build my Church. And the gates of the underworld can never hold out against it. I will give you the keys of the kingdom of heaven: whatever you bind on earth shall be considered bound in heaven; whatever you loose on earth shall be considered loosed in heaven. (Mt. 16:16–20)

It is important to note that immediately following the Matthean passage quoted above comes a passage in which Jesus sternly rebukes Peter, and in fact, calls him "Satan":

> From that time on Jesus began to make it clear to his disciples that he was destined to go to Jerusalem and suffer grievously at the hands of the elders and chief priests and scribes, to be put to death, and to be raised up on the third day. Then, taking him aside, Peter started to remonstrate with him. "Heaven preserve you, Lord," he said, "this must not happen to you." But he turned and said to Peter, "Get behind me, Satan! You are an obstacle in my path, because the way you think is not God's way but man's." (Mt. 16:21–23)

Unless one is going to posit the absurd proposition that Jesus founded his Church on Satan and entrusted to Satan the keys of the kingdom of heaven, with the power to bind and loose, this rebuke of Jesus must mean that Peter's "counsel" to Jesus was contrary to the will of God, therefore earning from Jesus not praise, blessing, or authority, but identification with Satan. If one is to be consistent with these two Matthean texts, Peter is accorded preeminent praise because of his faith; but due to his lack of faith and his contradiction of the will of God, he receives an unparalleled rebuke.

From this, it is reasonable to conclude that Peter's "authority" is constituted by his faith in Jesus and by his living the will of God. This interpretation is supported by numerous other scriptural incidents in which Jesus equates goodness and "identity" with doing the will of God. A particularly powerful example of this is found in Mark 3:31–35, Matthew 12:46–50, and Luke 8:19–21: Jesus said, "Anyone who does the will of God, that person is my brother and sister and mother."

And two other scriptural passages have been cited in support of Peter's primacy over the other apostles. One is from the twenty-first chapter of John's Gospel, beginning at verse 15, where Jesus asks Peter three times if Peter loves him, and after each reply, Jesus tells Peter to feed his lambs. The meaning of this exchange is not that Jesus is now passing on the staff of his authority to Peter; it is, rather, that Jesus, the "good shepherd," who has sacrificed his life for his sheep (see John 10:7–18, 19:28–30), is now asking Peter, who has three times denied even knowing Jesus, whether he is willing to do the same. This twenty-first chapter in John is not about power, but about love and forgiveness.

The other is spoken during the last supper of Jesus with his apostles, where Jesus says:

> Simon, Simon! Satan, you must know, has got his wish to sift you all like wheat; but I have prayed for you, Simon, that your faith may not fail, and once you have recovered, you in your turn must strengthen your brothers. (Lk. 22:31–33)

Further, if Jesus did appoint Peter to be the leader of the apostles, with all the others subject to him, then neither Peter nor the other apostles honored this appointment. This is demonstrated in the following scriptural events.

Peter did not appoint the apostle who was to take the place of Judas. Matthias and Joseph were nominated by the community, who drew lots, and the lot fell to Matthew (Acts 1:15–26).

Peter was sent as an emissary with John to Samaria.

When the apostles in Jerusalem heard that Samaria had accepted the word of God, they sent Peter and John to them, and they went down there, and prayed for the Samaritans to receive the Holy Spirit. . . . (Acts 8:14–16)

If, in fact, Peter himself had had authority over the rest of the apostles, they would not have had the power to send Peter and John to the Samaritans. Peter would have sent them, not they him.

The apostle Paul publicly rebuked Peter (also called Cephas) for pretending to be in sympathy with the Jewish Christians who insisted that Gentile converts to Christianity be circumcized and abide by Mosaic laws:

When Cephas came to Antioch, however, I opposed him to his face, since he was manifestly in the wrong. His custom had been to eat with the pagans, but after certain friends of James arrived he stopped doing this and kept away from them altogether for fear of the group that insisted on circumcision. The other Jews joined him in this pretense, and even Barnabas felt himself obliged to copy their behavior.

When I saw they were not respecting the true meaning of the Good News, I said to Cephas in front of everyone, "In spite of being a Jew, you live like the pagans and not like the Jews, so you have no right to make the pagans copy Jewish ways." (Galatians 2:11–14)

It is evident from this rebuke that Paul did not consider Peter's authority definitive in this extremely important matter. Nor did the Christian Jews belonging to the party of the circumcision in Jerusalem regard Peter's authority as superior to theirs. They criticized him and called him to give an accounting of his association with the Gentiles who had been led to faith. In the eleventh chapter of Acts, verses 1–18, Peter explains his actions to his critics.

Regarding Question 3

The words and actions of Jesus do not indicate that he intended to establish a hierarchical authority. Jesus could have chosen his apostles from among the Levites, priests, and high priests of the Temple; he did not do so. He could have chosen his apostles from among the rabbis, Pharisees, and Sadducees; he did not do so. Whenever the apostles argued over who among themselves was the greatest, Jesus tried to teach them a totally different concept of greatness and authority.

"What were you arguing about on the road?" They said nothing because they had been arguing which of them was the greatest. So he sat down, called the Twelve to him, and said, "If anyone wants to be first, he must make himself last of all and servant of all." (Mk. 9:34–36)

An argument started between them about which of them was the greatest. Jesus knew what thoughts were going through their minds, and he took a little child and set him by his side and then said to them, "Anyone who welcomes this little child in my name welcomes me; and anyone who welcomes me welcomes the one who sent me. For the least among you all, that is the one who is great." (Lk. 9:46–48)

The Gospels of Mark and Matthew relate the attempt by James and John to obtain from Jesus positions of power when his messiahship was recognized. The other apostles became jealous and angry over this, and Jesus reprimanded them all:

James and John, the sons of Zebedee, approached him, "Master," they said to him, "we want you to do us a favor." He said to them, "What is it you want me to do for you?" They said to him, "Allow us to set one at your right hand and the other at your left in your glory." "You do not know what you are asking," Jesus said to them. "Can you drink the cup that I must drink, or be baptized with the baptism with which I must be baptized?" They replied, "We can." Jesus said to them, "The cup that I must drink you shall drink, and with the baptism with which I must be baptized you shall be baptized, but as for seats at my right hand or my left, these are not mine to grant; they belong to those to whom they have been allotted."

When the other ten heard this they began to feel indignant with James and John, so Jesus called them to him and said to them, "You know that among the pagans their so-called rulers lord it over them, and their great men make their authority felt. This is not to happen among you. No; anyone who wants to become great among you must be your servant, and anyone who wants to be first among you must be slave to all. For the Son of Man himself did not come to be served but to serve, and to give his life as a ransom for many." (Mk. 10:35–45)

In the Gospel of Luke, this dispute among the apostles repeated itself even at the time of the last Passover meal Jesus was to share with his friends:

A dispute arose also between them about which of them was to be regarded as the greatest. And he said to them, "The kings of the Gentiles exercise lordship over them; and those in authority over them are called benefactors. This must not happen with you. No, the greatest among you must behave as if he were the youngest, the leader as if he were the one who serves. For who is the greater, the one at the table or the one who serves? The one at table, surely, Yet here I am among you as one who serves." (Lk. 22:24–27)

In the Gospel of John, Jesus performs the ministratlons of a slave or servant in washing the feet of his apostles.

"Do you understand," he said, "what I have done to you? You call me Master and Lord, and rightly, so I am. If I, then, the Lord and Master, have washed your feet, you should wash one another's feet. I have given you an example so that you may copy what I have done." (Jn. 13:13–15)

The apostle Paul praises this quality of Jesus, his willingness to become the slave and servant of all, even to the point of sacrificing his own life:

His state was divine, yet he did not cling to his equality with God but emptied himself to assume the condition of a slave, and became as men are; and being as all men are, he was humbler yet, even to accepting death, death on a cross. (Phil. 2:6–8)

Jesus' life and death totally challenged the notions of authority current in his day. The Messiah was expected to restore Israel to a position of spiritual and temporal supremacy. Yet Jesus was crucified as a criminal, his followers caused a schism in Judaism, and the Temple that was the House of God and the glory and promise of Israel was destroyed by Rome. Although Jesus was a Jew, he disregarded some of the Mosaic customs and rituals of his time, setting himself and his disciples above the law.[34] Jesus frequently castigated the religious authorities, accusing them of being hypocrites, whitened sepulchres, and sons of the devil.[35] He fled from people trying to make him king;[36] refused to be swept up in the hatred of Roman rule;[37] and claimed authority over the Temple[38] by driving out the money changers and by promising to "rebuild," in three days, the "temple" of his crucified body. Further, he boldly informed the high priest that his authority came from God.[39]

The many cures that Jesus performed on the Sabbath demonstrated that he thought the Sabbath had been created for man, not man for the Sabbath.[40] Jesus' authority emanated precisely from his living out of God's will. This was his food,[41] his sustenance, and his abiding concern. And what did Jesus understand God's will to be? Proclaiming the reign of God, liberating from the bondage of sin, healing, feeding the hungry, clothing the naked, and comforting the afflicted and the lonely. It was this wholly consuming love for people and for God that generated the power and charism of Jesus' authority. His "teaching made a deep impression on the people because he taught them with authority, and not like their own scribes."[42]

Jesus inspired his apostles, his disciples, and anyone whom he met to realize this same authority, this same reign of God, within themselves. This was not a hierarchy possessed according to "office" and fullness of the "power of orders." Jesus commanded his disciples to bring this Good News to all nations.[43] He wanted everyone to know God's will, love, compassion, forgiveness, and healing in themselves. Jesus revealed that God's love is the birthright of all, not the dominion of a few. And the responsibility of proclaiming this truth was likewise the joyful mandate of all who have known God.

QUESTIONS REGARDING WHETHER
ECCLESIAL AUTHORITY, IN ITS SOLEMN TEACHING,
IS DIVINELY ASSISTED BY THE HOLY SPIRIT
AND HENCE INFALLIBLE AND WORTHY OF
COMPLETE OBEDIENCE: A BIBLICAL PERSPECTIVE

Jesus directed his apostles to proclaim the kingdom of heaven, cure the sick, raise the dead, cleanse the lepers, and cast out devils, assuring them, "anyone who welcomes you welcomes me; and those who welcome me welcome the one who sent me." He also assured the apostles not to worry about what to say during their trials before religious and political authorities, "because it is not you who will be speaking; the Spirit of your Father will be speaking in you."[44]

**Do These Assurances Mean that the Apostles,
in Their Judgments Regarding Faith and Morals,
Were Infallible and Worthy of Full Obedience?**

The apostles performed great deeds in Jesus' name, and many of them suffered martyrdom because of their love for him. But Scripture also records faith and moral judgments on their part that were quite fallible and unworthy of obedience. They constantly bickered among themselves as to who would have the most power when Jesus' messianic reign was finally established. Peter told Jesus that He would not have to suffer. Judas betrayed Him and then hanged himself. Peter, who had promised that he would die for Jesus, denied even knowing him. And when Jesus was arrested, all the Apostles abandoned him. And most of them, after the women testified that Jesus had risen from the dead, refused to believe. Apostolic activity, even after the Pentecost experience described in the second chapter of Acts, was rife with arguments. Examples of this are found in Acts 11, 15; 1 Corinthians 1, 3; 2 Corinthians 2; and Galatians 2.

The apostles were human beings with weaknesses and strengths. Their authority came not from themselves, or from the fact that they were invited by Jesus to proclaim the Gospel—it derived from following the Gospel by living according to Jesus' spirit of faith and love.

Jesus Said, "I Am the Way, the Truth, and the Life."
Does this Mean that "the Truth" Proclaimed about Jesus
by His Apostles, and Their Successors, Is Infallible,
Inerrant, and Irreformable?

Scripture attests to the fact that Jesus "grew in grace, wisdom, and age." He spent nearly three decades in obscurity before finally proclaiming the reign of God. From the very first day that Jesus began his public ministry, people began arguing over who he was and what he was saying. Jesus struggled mightily with his Father's will, even begging to be free of it; his last affirmation of faith was a cry of anguish, "My God, My God, why have you forsaken me?"

The Twelve, even as Jesus hung on the cross, did not truly know who he was. And in the post-Resurrection Church, after the disciples began finally, in the Holy Spirit, to proclaim the identity and gospel of Jesus, they constantly disputed what his message really meant, and how to apply it.

How, then, can a papacy nineteen and twenty centuries later claim to possess the infallible, irreformable truth about Jesus? If Jesus did not establish an authority based on apostolic succession and infallible doctrine worthy of full obedience, what kind of authority did he establish?

THE AUTHORITY INSPIRED BY JESUS

The words and actions of Jesus do not suggest that he established an authority founded on "apostolic succession" and doctrinal irreformability. But the words and actions of Jesus do prove very clearly that he inspired a radically new relationship with God.

The God Jesus proclaims is Abba, who embraces sinners, goes out in search of those who have strayed, protects the orphan and the widow, gives bread daily to the hungry, and watches over the birds of the air and the flowers of the field. Abba comforts those who mourn, blesses the peacemakers, the pure of heart, and those who hunger and thirst for justice. Abba rejoices more in the return of the prodigal than of those who have never been lost. Jesus' mission and identity are totally consumed with loving his Father, and with loving others as his Father does. This was Jesus' sustenance, his life, and it even motivated his journey to the cross. It was the spirit Jesus entrusted to his friends, the unique authority he gave his disciples: the same spirit that bound Jesus in love to Abba, bound him in turn in love to them, and he gave this spirit to his disciples, so that they, too, would love Abba and their neighbor as Jesus did. "This is my commandment: love one another as I have loved you" (Jn. 15:12). This was the authority Jesus gave to all who chose to follow him. He did not establish an institution based on rank and inerrancy, but an authority emanating from the spirit in him passionately to love God and neighbor.

How far is this obedience from that demanded by the Church hierarchy? The hierarchy demands obedience to apostolic successors and to the infallible, irreformable truths solemnly defined by the pope. The obedience Jesus asks for has nothing to do with dominion or submission or one person's judgment being more godlike than another's: all he asks is that we be faithful to his spirit.

HIERARCHICAL AND INFALLIBLE AUTHORITY: PASTORAL PERSPECTIVES

Even though the evolving structure of authority in the Catholic Church has survived the Roman Empire, the Dark Ages, the Reformation, the Enlightenment, and two World Wars—and even though Roman Catholic authority has contributed susbstantially to world civilization and to the progress of humanity—its hierarchical and infallible authority should be seriously reexamined. These characteristics must be called into question not only because their biblical justifications have been shown to be extremely dubious, but also because their specific historical origins are fraught with confusion, ambiguity, and strife.

Yes, the papacy and the Magisterium have borne the scars of nineteen centuries of heresies and false doctrines advocating everything from God is dead,[45] to denial of Christ's identity,[46] to Satanic worship, to group sex,[47] to castration,[48] to hatred of marriage[49] and everything material, to masochistic ascetisicm,[50] and frenetic expectation of the apocalypse.[51] And yes, many in the Church have shed their blood and their lives to affirm one truth: Jesus, not Caesar, is Lord. Further, the papacy and the bishops, after the collapse of the Roman Empire, fed the starving and carried the besieged remnants of Western civilization through the Dark Ages.[52] And granted, the best of the monastic zeal for imitating Christ became the soil from which sprang love for Scripture and spiritual wisdom; a more vigorous and inspiring spirituality; reforming popes; and some of the greatest teachers in history, including Bernard of Clairveaux, St. Francis of Assisi, Thomas Aquinas, Thomas à Kempis, St. Teresa of Avila, and St. John of the Cross. But all these glories and all these scars and struggles were not adequate justification for placing the papacy (and the Magisterium) above the human condition in declaring it infallible.

Papal infallibility, solemnly defined only in the latter half of the nineteenth century, occasioned the excommunication of Germany's leading theologian, Ignaz Dollinger. Further, the infallibility doctrine caused a schism in those countries opposing it: Germany, Austria, Switzerland, and the Netherlands.[53] It has since become a stumbling block to ecumenical unity and a scandal to persons everywhere who sense in the spirit of this definition dissonance with the spirit of Jesus, who "grew in grace, wisdom, and age"[54]; who taught frequently in parables; who confessed that he did not know the day or the hour of the final days;[55] who knew the anguish of doubt and dread in Gethsemane;[56] who tasted despair in the betrayal and abandonment[57] of his friends; and who, in the unfathomable cry from the cross for his God, experienced the absolute limits of human agony.[58] This definition of papal infallibility ignores the sins and frailties of Peter —the "stone on whom the Church is built"—who, even after Pentecost, compromised what he knew to be God's will regarding Mosaic practices and the Gentile Christians.[59]

What good are infallible definitions when the life of a Christian is primarily one of faith, not certitude? What good is it to turn definitions into truths, truths into banners of Inquisition[60] and Conquest[61]—to turn the truths of Christ into swords to slay dissenters and disbelievers? Have we learned so little from the Crusades and the flaming corpses of the "heretics"; so little from the Man whose greatest and only commandment was love?

Pope Boniface VIII, in his bull *Unam Sanctam,* foreshadowed the dangerous extreme of papal primacy and hierarchical authority when he stated "that to be subject to the Roman pontiff is necessary for salvation." In the same bull he explains why the authority of kings is subject to the authority of the Church:

> He who denies that the temporal sword is in the power of Peter, misunderstands the word of the Lord, "Put up thy sword unto the sheath." Both are in the power of the Church, the spiritual and the material. But the latter is to be used for the Church, the former by her; the former by the priest, the latter by kings and captains, but at the will and by the permission of the priest. The one sword, then, should be under the other, and temporal authority subject to spiritual.[62]

Pope Boniface VIII was unequivocally telling King Philip of France and all other civil rulers that they derived their authority to rule from God through the pope.*

"Infallible" authority obstructs the human instinct to know by claiming inerrant, irreformable truth. This dynamic tendency toward ever greater knowledge and understanding of truths is severely abridged by the static nature of "irreformable truth." Infallible authority limits personal freedom by demanding assent of mind, will,

---

*While a thorough historical analysis lies outside the scope of this chapter, it would prove very instructive to examine the evolution of the concepts of hierarchical authority and primacy as articulated by Popes Siricius, Leo IX (who excommunicated Patriarch Michael Cerularius during the Great Schism of 1054), Gregory II, Innocent III, Boniface VIII, Pius IX, and the rivaling popes of the Western Schism (1378–1417), who represented three simultaneous claims to the papacy; three different papal Sees; and three different papal obediences, each excommunicating all those not following its claim. During this schism, the entire Church had been declared excommunicated.

and soul, even though the faithful may have pressing and unanswered questions about the "declaration." Such authority disturbs the intellectual process, where choices flow naturally from knowledge that has been assimilated from within, not imposed by external dictates. It further limits human freedom by asserting that its authority is divinely willed, and therefore to be obeyed, even when it is not fully understood. Such authority creates tension between the "divine will" and the uninformed human will. To demand human assent on the basis that such assent is willed by God is to imply either that God is willing to force human freedom, or that human freedom, upon knowing God or truth, would not eagerly welcome such wisdom.

To assert that God wills infallible knowledge to issue from one man, in virtue of his papal office, leads to the untenable conclusion that divine wisdom is the prerogative of the Holy See, and not the grace given to all who love God. If ecclesial authority is, indeed, hierarchical and infallible, the "locus" of the Christ-experience must shift from the human heart to the human institition.

According to hierarchical authority, it is the institution, and those holding office in that institution (pope, cardinals, bishops, priests, and deacons) who represent, in descending order, Christ's healing, inspiring, and guiding action. In this model of authority, the prime teacher, sanctifier, and shepherd is the pope, the one closest to the Truth, hence the one most capable of articulating infallibly the faith and morals of Christians throughout the world. After the pope come his cardinals and bishops assembled in council, or acting, each in his own diocese, in the place of Christ or the Magisterium. In this model of authority, the holiest blessing is the apostolic blessing, the lowliest that of a lay person. The hierarchy decides who is a true or a false believer, a true or a false teacher. And because the hierarchy are the sanctifiers and the guardians of the truth, those who dissent from it are regarded as evil and perpetrators of error.

This means that nearly one billion Catholics, in matters of faith and morals, have no authority to govern their own lives; that decisions regarding faith, divorce and remarriage, birth control, and ethical conduct are to be mandated from above rather than determined from within. Such authority, determined by the principle of apostolic succession and not by the promise God made to write his law on the hearts of all who love him, leaves most of the Church out in the cold, voiceless in those decisions which are intended to direct the course of their faith and moral conduct.

In the light of this, and of the frequent warnings of Jesus to his jealous, power-conscious apostles, what would be the warnings of Jesus today to those who consider "authority" as spiritual power vested in a principle of apostolic succession, hierarchy, and measures of fullness from the lowliest lay person to the office claiming supreme, full, immediate, and universal authority? While the principle of unity may indeed be served by the Church having a single leader, is it not alien to the spirit of Christ and the Gospels to suggest that a single leader (the pope) or a single institution (the Roman Catholic Church) or a single governing body (the Magisterium) has an exclusive claim to the authority of Christ? Does it really honor the humility of Jesus to assume titles such as "servant of the servants of God" while at the same time claiming universal, supreme, and jurisdictional authority over all the servants?

When Christ's authority is claimed as an exclusive, infallible, and hierarchical endowment, Catholicism becomes a religion not principally of encounter but of mediation. Sanctification is no longer experienced as God's will and miraculous love directly healing and vivifying the human heart, or as God's love directly infusing the community of human hearts; rather, holiness becomes contact with God through sacred ministers and rituals, holy places, and unquestioning obedience.

In this model of authority, the keys of the kingdom—the power of binding and loosing, of sanctifying, teaching, and governing— rest ultimately in the hands of the pope and the Magisterium, and are dispensed from their hands and will through the lower ranks of the hierarchy to the rest of the faithful. If we follow these principles of hierarchical and obediential submission to their logical conclusions, we see that personal salvation is dependent upon surrendering individual will to the voice of other human beings, who claim to be the voice of God. In short, salvation is no longer personal.

Such authority is inimical to the spirit of Christ and to the dignity of the human person. That it should occasion sorrow, consternation, divisiveness, and even rejection attests to that enduring spirit in humankind that senses itself as radically free and radically capable of the most fundamental of all human choices, the choice to love or to reject God.

The exclusion of nearly all Catholics from the governing process of the Church, the ever expanding suppression of intellectual, moral, and theological questioning, the widening chasm between what the hierarchy teach and what the faithful do, the stern warnings of Jesus to his apostles to serve rather than to rule, and, finally, the mere existence of countless Christians who are living and dying while witnessing to their love for God and each other—these alone should be reasons enough for the hierarchical Church humbly and definitively to leave behind all claims to infallibility as well as all claims to spiritual ascendency justified only by apostolic succession.

In the realm of faith, there can be no such thing as infallible, inerrant, irreformable definitions. Faith, more than any other form of human cognition, requires humility—a radical and dynamic openness to God, who is at once revelation and mystery. In the ministry of Jesus, whose spirit feeds the hungry, clothes the naked, gives sight to the blind, and sets the captives free, the only primacy is that of love.

NOTES

1. Authority pervades every aspect of daily life: familial, social, educational, religious, economic, and political. It seems crucially important to have a clear understanding of its nature, meaning, kinds, values, abuses, and limits. Authority as an office is often defined as legal or rightful power to command obedience; authority as a person is defined as an individual, group, or personified code possessing such power. What these definitions (and philosophies, religions, and politics deriving from them) lack is precisely the relational nature of authority. Laws, ethics, and codes which societies ignore or rebel against may possess a "notional" authority, but certainly not

a "praxis" authority, i.e., one realized in deeds and action. What is needed is a definition of authority that realizes its dynamic relational nature.

Moreover, a definition of authority by office alone, or by entitlement to power, is an indication of institutional origins. But such definitions do not address how these institutions are validated. This book reflects a twelve-year exploration into the essense of authority—an attempt to discover a definition of authority so basic that it might serve as a criterion for evaluating all forms of human authority. This chapter focuses principally on religious authority in the Catholic tradition.

2. *New York Times,* November 25, 1985.

3. *The Catholic Priest in the United States,* dir. A. Greeley (Washington, D.C.: Publications Office, United States Catholic Conference, 1972), pp. 205–207.

4. J. Zwack, *Annulment: Your Chance to Remarry Within the Catholic Church* (New York: Harper & Row, 1983).

5. *New York Times,* September 4, 1985; *National Catholic Reporter,* September 6, 1985.

6. G. Thomas, *Desire and Denial* (Boston: Little, Brown & Co., 1986), p. 12.

7. For the published text of the January 1989 Cologne Declaration, see the March 17, 1989 issue of the *National Catholic Reporter.*

8. Two principles frequently asserted by the papacy concerning its authority are its primacy and its infallibility. Ignatius of Antioch's salutation in his epistle to the Church of Rome is thought to be the earliest avowal of the primacy of Rome written by a non-Roman ecclesiastic. See J. Quasten, *Patrology* (Westminster, Md.: Newman Press, 1950), 1: 65–69.

Irenaeus in *Adv. Haer.* (3, 3, 2 and 3, 3, 3) says the preeminence of the Church of Rome is established in that it was founded "by the two most glorious apostles Peter and Paul," and that this Church, through apostolic succession and efficient leadership, has faithfully preached the truth of the Christian faith. See F. X. Funk, *Der Primat der römischen Kirche nach Ignatius und Irenaeus: Kirchengeschichtliche Abhandlungen und Untersuchungen* (Paderborn, 1897), 1: 1–23. But J. McCue emphasizes caution in taking Irenaeus's statement to mean a Roman primacy. See J. McCue, "Roman Primacy in the First Three Centuries," *Concilium* 4, no. 7 (April 1971): 40–41.

In writing about the unity of the Church, Cyprian asserts the equality of honor and power among the apostles, but whose unity, willed by Christ himself, originates in the one rock, Peter. See Mt. 16:18 and Cyprian, *De ecclesiae unitate,* in C. Thornton, *Library of the Church Fathers* (1839), 3: 131–52. But this statement must be read along with others Cyprian makes about the limits of Rome's power to legislate in his own diocese (see Epist. 59, 14; 71, 3; and CSEL 3, 1, 436).

For other statements supporting the primacy of Rome, see PL 13, 370 B; Mansi, IV, 1295-96; ACO, 1, 1, 3, 60; Sermo, III, 4, PL 54, 147 A; Epistola 30, PL 20, 590 A; PL 50, 485 A; Epistola 14, PL 54, 671 B; Epistola 10, 2, PL 54, 650 A; Epistola 14, 1, PL 54, 671 B; Epistola 14, PL 20, 777; PL 54, 141–56; Sermo 82, PL 54, 422–24; ACO 11, 1, 2, 93; Mansi, VII, 9; ACO 11, 1, 2, 141; Mansi, VII, 135-36; ACO 11, 1, 65; Mansi, VI, 580; ACO 1, 11, 12; Mansi, IV, 1036 A; ACO 1, 11, 22; Mansi, IV, 1292 D. See also, chapters 20–35 in Athanasius's *Apologia contra Arianos,* in the *Library of the Fathers of the Holy Catholic Church* translated by M. Atkinson, edited by E. B. Pusey, J. Keble, and J. H. Newman (Oxford, 1843), 13: 13–124; DS, esp. 3053–3075.

9. DV2, p. 38.

10. P. Fransen, *A Short History of the Meaning of the Formula "Faith and Morals,"* as Found in Hermeneutics of the Councils and Other Studies, collected by H. Mertens and F. De Grave (Leuven University Press, 1985), pp. 287–318; DV2, pp. 47–50.

11. DV2, p. 48.

12. Ibid., p. 49; Mansi, 52, 1215 CD, 1216-17 A; Mansi, 52, 1213.

13. DV2, pp. 42–52, pars. 22–27.

14. Ibid., pp. 37, 38, par. 18.

15. Ibid., pp. 37–38.

16. Ibid., p. 43.

17. Ibid., pp. 48, no. 25.

18. Ibid., pp. 48–49.

19. Ibid., p. 40, no. 21.

20. I Cor. 9 and 15; Gal. 1:16; Rom. 1:4–5; I Thess. 2:2–4. See also: J. Knox, "Rom. 15:14–33 and Paul's Conception of His Apostolic Mission," *Journal of Biblical Literature* 83 (1964): 1–11; J. Munck, "Paul, the Apostles and the Twelve," *Studia Theologica* 3 (1949): 96–110; J. Crocker, "The Apostolic Succession in the Light of the History of the Primitive Church," *Anglican Theological Review* 18 (1936): 1–21; and "Apostolic Succession," in *Concilium,* Hans Kung, ed. (New York: Paulist Press, 1968), 34: esp. 5–51.

21. Lk. 1:46–55.
22. Lk. 1:42–45.
23. Lk. 2:22–35.
24. Lk. 2:36–38.
25. Mt. 3:1–12; Mk. 1:1–8; Lk. 3:1–18; Jn. 1:19–34.
26. Jn. 1:1–42.
27. Lk. 8:26–39; Mk, 5:1–20; Mt. 8:28–34.
28. Jn. 12:1–8; Mk. 14:3–9; Mt. 26:6–13.
29. Jn. 9:1–41.
30. Lk. 17:11–19.
31. Mt. 15:21–28: Mk. 7:24–30.
32. Lk. 7:1–10; Mt. 8:5–13.
33. Lk. 24:9–11; Mk. 16:1–8; Jn, 20:1–18; Mt. 28:1–10.
34. Mt. 12:1–8; Mk. 2:23–28; Lk. 6:1–5.
35. Jn. 8:33–47.
36. Jn. 6:1–15.
37. Mt. 22:15–22; Mk. 12:13–17; Lk. 20:20–26.
38. Mt. 21:12–17; Jn. 2:13–22; Lk. 19:45–46; Mk. 11:15–19.
39. Jn. 19:8–11; Mt. 26:57–68; Lk. 22:66–71.
40. Mt. 12:9–14; Mk. 3:1–6; Lk. 6:6–11.
41. Jn. 4:34.
42. Mt. 7:28–29.
43. Mt. 28:16–20; Mk. 16:16–18.
44. Mt. 10:1–42.
45. Friedrich Nietzsche, *Thus Spoke Zaruthustra; "Is God Dead?"* *Concilium,* J. Metz, ed. (New York: Paulist Press, 1966), 16, esp.: G. Fessard, "The Theological Structure of Marxist Atheism," A. Bourneuf, trans., pp. 7–24; P. Ricoeur, "The Atheism of Freudian Psychoanalysis," R. Dowd, trans., pp. 59–72; and I. Fetscher, "Developments in the Marxist Critique of Religion," R. Brennan, trans., pp. 131–54.
46. There are many misconceptions concerning Jesus's identity:

  a) that he is pure myth and never really existed;

  b) that he was not the Messiah foretold by Scripture;

  c) that he was man but not the son of God;

  d) that he was God but not really man;

e) that he became the Messiah only after his baptism, or only after his death on the cross;

f) that his message was exclusively political, or sociological, or eschatological.

See Gregory Nanzianzus, Ep. 101, 4–6, and J. Knox, *The Humanity and Divinity of Christ* (Cambridge University Press, 1967).

47. The Nicolites were purported to be followers of Nicolas, a deacon of the early Church who had offered his wife, whom he loved with too excessive a passion, to his fellow deacons for their sexual pleasure. See H. Lea, *History of Sacerdotal Celibacy* (New Hyde Park, N.Y.: University Books, 1966), pp. 15–16.

48. As a sign of his total commitment to conquering the lusts of the body, Origen castrated himself. And though he did not advocate this for others, there is said to have been a sect called the Valesians who inflicted castration. See Lea, *History of Sacerdotal Celibacy* p. 21.

49. The Manicheans, the Gnostics, and the Excalceati advocated shunning marriage as evil.

50. Among others, the Encratites, the Marcionites, Abstinentes, Manicheans, Flaggelantes, and the Jansenists.

51. Apocalyptic writings, anonymously ascribed to Abraham, Jacob, Moses, Baruch, Daniel, and Ezra, may have had some influence on the thinking of John the Baptist, Jesus, Paul, and John the Evangelist. Apocalyptic consciousness expects the soon-to-be-realized total reign of God, the consummation of the world, and the end of time. Over the last two thousand years there have been groups of millenarianists expecting an apocalyptic fulfillment of God's reign of earth, among them the Montanists, the fifteenth-century Taborites, the seventeenth-century Quakers, the Mormons, and the Jehovah's Witnesses.

52. G. Baum, "Doctrinal Renewal," *Journal of Ecumenical Studies* 2, no. 3 (1965): 365–81; G. Baum, "The Question of Infallibility," *Journal of Ecumenical Studies* 4, no. 1 (1965): 124ff.

53. Hans Kung, *Infallible? An Inquiry,* E. Quinn, trans. (New York, Doubleday & Co., 1971), p. 101.

Other statements causing serious concern and divisiveness:

If anyone says that the Holy Apostle Peter has not been constituted by Christ, the Lord, as the leader of all the apostles and as the visible head of the Church Militant, or that he has received only a primacy of honor and not a primacy of true and proper jurisdiction (supreme administrative power) from our Lord Jesus Christ directly and immediately, let him be anathema. (DS 3055.)

Instituted by Christ, and hence by divine right, Peter has an unbroken line of successors to his universal primacy. The bishop of Rome is this successor. (Briefly summarized in DS 3058.)

54. Lk. 2:39–40.

55. Mt. 24:1–36.

56. Mt. 26:36–46; Mk. 14:32–42; Lk. 22:40–46.

57. Mt. 26:56; Mk. 14:50–51.

58. Mk. 15:33–34; Mt. 27:45–50.

59. R. Bellarmine, *De summo pontifice* (Ingolstadt, 1586–1593; Paris, 1870), Book II, chapter 29, I, 607.

60. Protecting the Christian faithful from error was the purpose of the Inquisition. Its methods were questionable: lives were often wrecked, books were burned, and prominent thinkers were silenced. Two of the more notable victims were Galileo and Giordano Bruno, who was burned at the stake in the Campo dei Fiori in 1600.

61. For the Crusades, and in particular, the centuries-long persecution of the Jews, see Kung, *Infallible? An Inquiry,* pp. 168–69.

62. Boniface VIII, *Unam Sanctam,* as quoted in C. Cary-Elwes, *Law, Liberty, and Love* (New York: Devin-Adair Co., 1951), p. 168. In his *Dictatus Papae,* Pope Gregory VII declared: "Only the Roman pontiff deserves to be called universal" (2); "The pope is the only man whose feet all princes must kiss" (9); "His dictates may not be reformed by anyone and he alone can reform all others" (18) "The pope may not be judged by anyone" (19); "The Roman Church has never erred and, as the Scriptures affirm, it cannot err" (22); "The Roman pontiff, if he has been canonically ordained, becomes holy without a doubt, through the merits of St. Peter" (23).

See also "The Concepts of 'Ecclesia' and 'Christianitas' and Their Relation to the Idea of Papal 'Plenitudo Potestatis' from Gregory VII to Boniface VIII," in *Miscell. Hist. Pontif.* 18 (1954): 49–77.

Part Three

Authority and Priesthood:

Personal Reflections and Decisions

Introduction

Part One of this volume, taking a sociological perspective, investigated the Church's policy on the exclusion of women and married clergy from the priesthood. Our analysis led to the following conclusions:

1) There is substantial disagreement between Church policy and the attitudes of Catholic laity, priests, and bishops.

2) The considered judgment of many North American bishops is that Christ's teachings, the mission of the Church, and the pastoral needs of the faithful would be better served by a priesthood that includes celibacy and marriage, women and men.

3) The Vatican's Sacred Congregation for Religious and the Superior General of the Jesuit Order regard it as consonant with "holy obedience" and the mind of Christ to suppress the attitudes of American bishops and the cardinals worldwide on priestly ministry.

4) Pope John Paul II defines the Church as a "theocratic institution, not a democracy," and will not take into consideration either a married clergy or the ordination of women.

Part Two examined the canons mandating celibacy for priests and "maleness" for ordination. Investigating these canons from biblical, historical, and ethical perspectives, we arrived at the following conclusions:

1) Imposing continence on married clergy was a violation of the marriage bond, the Ninth Commandment, and the explicit will of Christ: "What God has joined, let no man divide."

2) Requiring priests, by law, to remain celibate is a violation of nature, both human and divine; an affront to the unitive love of God as revealed in conjugal love; and a vitiation of the purpose of law.

3) Exclusion of women from ordination based on gender alone insults the dignity of Christian women, contradicts the image of God and Christ revealed in women and men living out lives of faith and love, and threatens the credibility of the Church's sacraments.

Part Two also examined, from a biblical perspective, two prevailing notions of Church authority: primacy and infallibility. Its analysis led to the conclusion that the authority Jesus entrusted was defined not by power and inerrancy, but by faith and love.

Confronted with the division between Church policy and Church attitudes, and the conflict between ecclesiastical and divine authority, we are prompted to ask how to respond to this crisis. Claiming either that the will of the Church, in a theocracy, is irrelevant, or that primacy and infallibility are divinely willed immediately establishes a chasm between the faithful and God. Under this claim anyone whose faith and morals are not wholly consonant with the mind of the Holy See is to that extent less a Catholic. And anyone who challenges the legitimacy of this authority is regarded as misinformed and contentious.

Calling for change within a milieu of hierarchy and inerrancy is to invite an immediate reprimand. Some Catholics, overwhelmed with the crises and despairing of ever changing a 2,000-year-old institution entrenched in exclusive power and certitude, have abandoned the Church. Others, realizing that faith is more a matter of a special relationship with God and the community than strict adherence to the institutional forms of religion, suffer silently. They wait patiently for the day when Church leaders and laws will come closer to manifesting the spirit of Christ already experienced in their hearts. Still others are convinced that Jesus did endow the papacy with primacy and infallibility, and that the current policy excluding marriage and women from the priesthood is precisely what Jesus intended.

As the problems of the priesthood and Church authority grow more disturbing, it becomes all the more expedient for individual Christians to choose a course of action. Nearly 2,500 years ago, the Greek playwright Sophocles concluded that individual will and not divine force determined the nature of human tragedy. With this insight, he sought to free humankind from the bondage of fate and the whims of quarreling gods. It seems a greater tragedy that the same Church, which was inspired by a man who fed the hungry, raised the dead, and set captives free, is now subjected to men who claim God bestowed on them their rank and their infallibility. Bondage to the whims of the gods or to the divine claims of human "authority" lead to the same end: subservience and oppression.

Part Three of this book and its appendices present the author's personal reflections and decisions regarding authority and priestly ministry.

8

Toward a More Natural Authority

"Deep within them I will plant my Law, writing it on their hearts. Then I will be their God and they shall be my people. There will be no further need for neighbor to try to teach neighbor, or brother to say to brother, 'Learn to know Yahweh!' No, they will all know me, the least no less than the greatest—it is Yahweh who speaks. . . ."
Jer. 31:33-34

Any historical or contemporary study of society will reveal various forms of authority, be they political or religious. Though the separation of political and religious authorities has, over the last several centuries, become increasingly pronounced, history reveals examples where the powers of religion and of politics were combined in a single authority. We may cite specific instances where certain political reigns endorsed a specific creed as the religion of the land, to the exclusion of all others. Examples abound of political leaders claiming authority directly from God; conversely, many religious leaders have claimed that their power came at the behest of the people. Even granting the vast differences between religious and political authorities, the fact remains that all of them are concerned with one thing: governance of human beings.

The previous chapter alluded briefly to the similarities between papal "infallibility" and the "nuclear authority" of recent U.S. and Soviet presidents. It evaluated infallibility and hierarchy from a biblical perspective, and concluded that the authority Jesus inspired was concerned with neither of these; rather, it emanated directly from loving God and others as Jesus himself did, and from faith in him as the Messiah. Chapter 5 described the confusion, anguish, and injustice generated by a Catholic hierarchical and canonical structure that has lost sight of the authority revealed by Jesus. Returning now to the parallels between religious and political authorities, we need look no further than the massacre in Tiananmen Square and the collapse of Soviet communism, to realize that political authority gone awry has also imposed crushing hardships on the people.

It is important to realize that both religious and political authority fail whenever the real needs of the people they are meant to serve are not met. It seems that this failure, common to both forms of authority, is more than accidental; it may be ascribed to the fact that the only denominator common to all forms of authority is this: people. To understand authority, therefore, we must understand human nature. Chapters 5 and 6 explored "human nature" from a biblical viewpoint. Here we shall complement that exploration with insights gleaned from psychology and philosophy.

It is not our intention, however, to advocate the supremacy of any particular political or religious system. Nor is it the purpose of this book to attempt to define a specific model of either political or religious authority. What we intend here is to try to discover the structural essence of authority, one so harmonious with human nature that its exercise generates not exclusivity, oppression, or chaos, but peace, freedom, and equality.

HUMAN AUTHORITY: WHAT IS IT?

To understand the essence of human authority, it is necessary first to understand the dynamic nature of the human person.

The most radical instincts of human nature are: the instinct to live, the instinct to know, and the instinct to love. These instincts are dynamically interrelated. Without life, knowledge and love are impossible; without knowledge, life and love are incomprehensible; without love, life and knowledge are void of desire, feeling, joy, or ecstasy. Life generates the very possibility, the "vital breath," of knowledge and love. Knowing generates consciousness of life and love, and the discernment that distinguishes lesser forms of life and love from greater. Loving generates union within the instincts, which in turn gives birth to more life, more knowing, more loving.

As powerful as these instincts are, however, and as determinative as they are of human activity, they are not absolutes, either individually, or in their interrelations, or taken as a whole. A power resides in the human person that is substantially shaped by these three instincts; but this power also shapes them. It is a power that permeates all the instincts; and all the instincts permeate this power. Its very existence depends upon the instincts; but it is also so absolute that it can terminate its own instincts. It is that power most frequently described as "human freedom," the absolutely radical ability to say yes or no to life, knowledge, and love.

This freedom does not beget human instincts, nor does it create life, knowledge, or love. Human freedom is that power which either affirms or negates those instincts. It is that precise ability in the body, mind, and heart of the human person to affirm or to deny his or her very being. By assenting to the natural course of the instincts, human freedom enhances them; by denying the natural course of the instincts, it diminishes them.

Thus, the most fundamental elements of human nature consist of the instincts to live, to know, and to love; human freedom, which radically affirms or denies the instincts; and, finally, the "I" (the personality or identity), which uniquely distinguishes each person. A person's instincts acquire, from infancy on, ever greater complexity as they interact, both among themselves and with the world at large. People whose instincts and freedom have been realized to a significant degree—we may name Abraham, Gotama, Confucius, Jesus, Mohammed, and Gandhi among them—are those who have inspired others, instilled confidence and admiration, and created "leadership."

As we shall see below, human authority is best understood by its radical consonance with maturely developed human nature.

"NATURAL" AUTHORITY AS THE ENERGY EMANATING FROM NATURE, RIGHTLY ORDERED

According to this understanding, authority originates in nature itself, and is validated by its consonance with it. Life, knowledge, and love generate authority; it is measured by the extent to which the instincts and human freedom have fulfilled themselves. Authority equals the energy of nature fulfilling itself in living well, knowing wisely, and loving completely. Authority equals energy times nature, or:

$$A = E \cdot N$$

But if nature is disordered, then the authority is disordered. If a person chooses to hate rather than love, then his authority to inspire or command others to love is totally undermined. Hence,

$$A- = E \cdot N-$$

If a person's intellectual talents are poorly developed, he is hardly in a position to teach others. If he has been lazy or careless about his health, he is not likely to be respected for any advice he might offer on physical fitness.

The radical measure of authority is determined by the degree to which a person has freely chosen to realize his or her fullest potential as a living, knowing, and loving being. This activity involves not only the self, but others and the world environment into which the self was born.

All authority, whether intrapersonal or interpersonal, involves three dynamic, relational elements:

1) the activity of nature, as it expresses itself

2) the natural subject of that activity

3) the natural object of that activity.

The energy of authority is a function of all three elements: if the activity is against the natural instincts, the resulting authority will be unnatural. If the subject exercising activity has misdirected or underdeveloped instincts, then the authority exercised will be misdirected and underdeveloped. If the object receiving the activity rebels against its own instincts, then even positively exercised authority will be negatively assimilated. However, when the instincts to live, know, and love are realized in act, in subject, and in object, then the energy realized in this authority is powerful both in intensity and extension.

Human authority, then, is "triadically relational" and emanates from human nature itself. As persons strive for survival, knowledge, and love, the very exercise of the instincts and of freedom generates an activity and a corresponding responsibility to that activity. As a carpenter is responsible for his building, as a mother is responsible for her baby, so is the human person responsible for the nurturing of her or his own instincts, powers, and actions.

Human authority is validated by its consonance with human nature and is concerned with the governance of all those things that directly affect human life, knowledge, love, freedom, and identity. Human authority, in virtue of its own nature, is intended to nurture all those things that enhance human life and to guard against all that threaten it. Such authority is most effective, and society is most tranquil, when those who govern, those who are governed, and the particular acts of governance are all in accord with human nature.

A human freedom or authority that would diminish or negate human nature is disordered and, in a manner proportional to the extent of its disorder, it loses its natural power to command the assent of others. Still, those governed retain the "freedom" to abide by such authority. In this instance, though it would not have the power of nature supporting it, disordered authority would nonetheless have the power of human choice confirming it. But such "authority" should not properly be termed authority at all, since its purpose is to negate human nature. The governing power emanating from it generates disturbance and chaos in society. The more the governed assent to disordered governance and governors, the greater the societal threat.

From this theory of natural authority, it is reasonable to conclude that when individuals or societies want to give correct external expression to the internal governing authority already operative within, the most effective models of authority (whether political or religious) would be those most in harmony with the properly ordered and triadically relational instincts of human nature. When both governor and governed act in a manner wholly consonant with their nature, then authority culminates in a society filled with vibrant life, wisdom, and love.

9

A Personal Declaration

"O Great Spirit, I raise my pipe to you, to your messengers the four winds, and to mother earth, who provides for our children. Give us the wisdom to teach our children to love, to respect, and to be kind to each other, so that they may grow with peace and mind. Let us learn to share all the good things that you provide for us on earth."
Prayer of John Pretty-on-Top, Crow Medicine Man,
at Assisi Peace Conference, October 27, 1986

On this Independence Day, 1986, prompted both by my faith in God and in the universally accepted notion that certain human rights —namely, to live, to know, and to love—are inalienable, I feel an inner urgency to say the following.

Both church and state, though separate, have the responsibility to nurture and protect these fundamental human rights. This is so because both are nothing more than the embodiment and articulation of individuals and groups associating because of common origin, need, or will. Any "church" or "state" that claims authority above and against the common good of its people, and in fact violates their basic human rights, is, to the specific extent of its violation, a lie. The long history of human travail, the oppression, the revolutions, the civil and international wars have demonstrated all too painfully the tragedy and havoc wrought by the breaching and trampling of these rights.

Church and state have the responsibility and the privilege to express, accompany, and govern human societies in their respectful wills to live more fully, know more clearly, and love more completely. Any "church" or "state" that denies or contradicts this fundamental dynamic and prerogative of human societies vitiates the very nature of church, state, and society.

All authorities, political and religious, are validated in light of their fostering and safeguarding this vital dynamic of human nature. Therefore, neither church nor state has the "authority" to compel anyone to do anything that is wrong. Nor has either the "authority" to order anyone to do anything that contradicts the fundamental rights of persons or societies. Neither church nor state has the power to frustrate, deny, or terminate the common good of its members. In those particular instances where individuals violate the rights of others or the common good, then it is the responsibility of the church or state, in virtue of the power given them by God, the faithful, and the citizenry to redress the violation swiftly and justly.

Further, the articulation of state and church into codes of laws, commandments, or morality is advantageous to the harmony and progress of societies as long as the code articulated is consonant with basic human rights. To the extent that this code denies these rights, it is to be redefined or rejected. To the extent that it becomes an "institution" unto itself, enforcing antiquated interpretations upon an oppressed society, likewise is it to be redefined or rejected. Codes are made for the well-being of people; people should not be made subject to or enslaved by codes. The multiple tragedies occasioned by the Inquisition, the Nuremberg trials, and the constant manipulation of codes to further greedy, inhumane, and criminal acts stand as somber witnesses to the cruelties and inhumanity perpetrated when human nature is made slave to a code—be it legal, constitutional, or religious.

This understanding of state, church, authority, and code as both validated and verified to the precise measure that each nurtures, guides, and protects fundamental human rights is a wisdom born out of human nature itself. This wisdom is not the exclusive domain of one state, church, or code; it is born out of the very hearts and minds of truth-seeking people in all countries, cultures, and religions. Religions and governments that order their people to despise or kill all those who do not accept "their truth" are false. To obey "orders" of this sort is to deny the very nature of humanity; it is to perpetuate "religions" and "governments" which are deceivers and destroyers. To obey "orders" of this sort is to undermine the very heart of society. The religious wars, the extermination of the Jews during the Second World War, the mass executions ordered by Stalin, the wholesale destruction of Indian tribes in the Americas, and the nuclear holocausts—all are bloody testaments to the cruelty, terror, and chaos unleashed when this wisdom is violated.

The records of human struggle, the rise and fall of civilizations both magnificent and corrupt prove humankind's incredibly creative and destructive potential. Societies mirror and embody human nature, a nature which can either nurture or destroy itself. At the very core, the very center, of all personal and societal activity there is the *choice* to know or to ignore, to love or to hate, to create life or to destroy it.

Now that society has evolved to the precarious position where one person, in a single choice, can unleash forces that would destroy humanity and literally shake the world from its axis, it is time for good-willed, life-affirming peoples of all cultures to disarm that power. Economic, political, and religious realities that have brought us to this brink of extinction are to be thoroughly reassessed and reevaluated in light of their radical choice to affirm or negate the basic human rights of societies both local and global. Choices purporting to affirm local human rights, even while negating the human rights of other states or nations, are a lie; choices that pretend to affirm the human rights of other nations or states, while denying local rights, are a lie.

A just society guarantees fundamental human rights for all. If, in political, ideological, and economic fact, governments would embody this self-evident truth, there would be no motive for *com-

petition resulting in rich nations living more extravagantly and luxuriously while poor nations starve. There would be no motive for ideological *conflict* resulting in churches and states plotting intrusion, subversion, conversion, or conquest. There would be no motive for *nuclear deterrence,* embodied in our present nuclear stockpiling, "Star Wars" strategies, and Mutually Assured Destruction (MAD). These "security measures" and "nuclear assurances" would be exposed for what they really are—a highly complex, multi-faceted, transnational web of human wants, secured by threatening other human beings. Thus, at the very core of mankind's "nuclear security" strategies lies a choice to see human nature itself as radically divided; to declare that some human beings are entitled to live, to know, and to love while others are not; to proclaim "I" rather than "You" or "We"; to pit one person against another; and to affirm "My freedom, my rights over yours!"—in short, a choice that, while seeking to preserve the self and the good one enjoys, will destroy another self and another good. This radical and fundamental choice can only lead to a human race divided against itself, seeking ever more powerful ways to preserve the self while destroying the other, from MAD missiles to international adversaries balancing the globe on the extremely fragile axis of threat and annihilation—in short, to *madness.*

Human choice is a gift given us in the very act of our creation. With it we can create families, states, churches, nations, and civilizations that respect, honor, and love all of creation, and every person in it by virtue of the common bond we all share as human beings. With that choice we can strive mightily to create a true global family, where the joys and triumphs, the failures and pain of one become the concern of all.

Our choices have brought us to the morning of a new age. State and church and code embody the best and worst of our choices. At this moment in history, at this turning point in our civilization, we are faced with the stark reality that our choices have created a technology which has the power to destroy this civilization, to put an end to all human choice forever. To bring us back from and beyond this madness, we must, each of us, make a choice for life, for "us," for the basic human rights of all peoples, nations, and cultures.

If this choice is made, dawn will blend freely and harmoniously with day and night, and our hearts and the hearts of our children will play and sleep peacefully. May God and all that us good in human nature bless us so.

10

A Brief Meditation on the Church in the Twenty-First Century

"When evening came, he was there alone, while the boat, by now far out on the lake, was battling with a heavy sea, for there was a head wind. In the fourth watch of the night he went towards them, walking on the lake, and when the disciples saw him walking on the lake they were terrified. 'It is a ghost,' they said, and cried out in fear. But at once Jesus called out to them, saying, 'Courage! It is I! Do not be afraid.' It was Peter who answered. 'Lord,' he said, 'if it is you, tell me to come to you across the water.' 'Come,' said Jesus. Then Peter got out of the boat and started walking toward Jesus across the water, but as soon as he felt the force of the wind, he took fright and began to sink. 'Lord! Save me!' he cried."

Mt. 14:23–31

So the cry of Peter becomes the cry of any one of us who has ever felt that ominous rush of terror, that sickening, heart-wrenching fear that death is about to drown us, swallow us, pull us down into darkness and void.

But death is not grave or casket: it is the scythe that divides living from not-living, knowing from not-knowing, loving from not-loving, believing from not-believing. It is that power each of us has to turn away from the face of the Lord and, instead, focus our atten-

179

tion on anything else—our lives, our fears, our importance, image, or authority.

As church authority flounders into the twenty-first century, asserting its primacy, apostolic succession, infallibility, and exclusive right to interpret Christ and his truth, it would be well to keep in mind this image of Peter, "the rock," crying out in sheer terror and sinking like a dead weight into an overwhelming sea. Until Church authority recognizes its mortality, its long heritage of human weakness, ambitions, failures, and sins, its procession of power and control will continue to scandalize and fragment and drown the faithful passengers who trusted the bark of Peter to lead them safely through the perils of life. Peter's greatness lay not in the gift he was given to heal, to forgive, and to speak in Jesus's name; his greatness lay, rather, in that he was loved by God and that he listened to the Spirit of God in his own heart and in the hearts of others. It was Peter's union with the word of God that enabled him to speak the Truth, and to love others even to the point of crucifixion.

If Church authority continues to idolize itself under the guise of proclaiming its sole proprietorship over the truth of Christ, then Church authority will sink deeper and faster than its rock did. If Church authority continues to insist on hierarchy and total assent, and to suppress all difference of opinion regarding faith and morals; if it defines these matters without the approval of the hundreds of millions of Catholics affected by these definitions, to regard all earthly authorities and politics as inferior, and to consider itself as the only real proclaimer of Truth—then Church authority is itself contributing to the division and chaos of the world.

If the Church is to survive, the "laity" must break free of the caste they have been placed in by the hierarchy. Catholics must recognize that every man and woman is created by God in God's own image, to live, to know, and to love—and that authority is the expression of this faith and love. This authority is the exclusive prerogative of no man, be he president or pope; rather, it is the birthright of all.

As this true consciousness of authority dawns in the Church, more and more will persons in office be selected because of their faith and love, and those in the institution will truly become servants. And more of the faithful, who had perceived themselves as sheep, will begin to recognize God's voice within their own hearts, and they will begin to prophesy and proclaim and heal. And eventually, the assembly will be not a hierarchy but a community.

In this Church of the twenty-first century, where women and men, married and celibate image the full Christ and gratefully accept all the responsibilities of discipleship, there will still be storms and still be times when Peter thinks he can, on his own authority, walk on the waters. The floundering Church will again need to reach out its hand and cry, "Lord, save me!" But we will be more aware that Peter is not only the pope, the bishop, or the priest; he is the Rock of Faith that is God's saving gift to each one of us who seeks, through love, to know the Truth.

No one is Lord but the Lord alone. Yet, through faith in that Lord, all of us become one, all of us image the One who is, who creates, and who loves.

Epilogue

Since entering the Jesuit Order in 1962, I have tried more clearly to understand what it means to be a priest and to do God's will. As a novice, I approached this inquiry with the thought that I could best help others find God and happiness if my own life as a priest were grounded in a love for Christ, in moral integrity, and in an intense desire to obey God's will as embodied in the voices of the pope, bishops, and my religious superiors.

In 1978, after I had completed all the requirements of Jesuit formation, it was expected that I would profess final vows of poverty, celibacy, and obedience. By then I had already ministered as a priest for five years and was very happy to have the privilege of helping others in their faith, their daily struggles, and their search for God. But as much as I loved the Jesuit community and the people whom I served as a priest, I found myself hesitant about making final vows. It was necessary to discover why.

After extensive reflection, I realized there had been many influences, both pastoral and personal, which prompted my hesitation. While I cannot elaborate on all those influences, it does seem germane to my purpose here to mention briefly some of the most important events that helped to shape my understanding of priesthood and authority.

VATICAN II: FROM AN ASCETIC
TO A UNITIVE SPIRITUALITY

Jesuit seminary training prior to Vatican II emphasized detachment from a sinful world, denial of self, and a strict disciplining of all affections and thoughts. The model for this spirituality was Jesus the celibate, the wandering preacher who had no place to lay his head; the misunderstood, despised, and crucified Christ. The dynamic of this spirituality was to purge oneself of original and personal sin, and to join Jesus in his battle to win souls back from the prince of this world and the powers of darkness. The daily routine of prayer, spiritual reading, silence, exhortation, and frequent examination of conscience all served to embody this ascetic spirituality.

After Vatican II, there was a radical shift—suddenly, the world was perceived as sacred. The Church was no longer characterized as an institution possessing exclusive, irreformable truths, but as a people of God on pilgrimage. Community and love became ever abiding themes. Prayer became communal. There were no more black vestments and Masses for the dead; these were replaced by white vestments and Masses of resurrection. Latin was out, the vernacular was in. The Mass, often in dialogue homilies, was presented as a Eucharistic celebration, not a sacrifice; the priest no longer faced the altar but the people. Jesus was proclaimed as companion, healer, and risen Lord. Instead of being defined as a purgative sacrifice, spirituality became instead a unitive celebration.

As grateful as I am for having experienced both spiritualities, this seemed to demonstrate that ideas, and their accompanying manifestations, could change radically. The temporary but profound disorientation caused by this change convinced me that ideas, especially those intimately affecting one's spirituality, should be carefully evaluated. The ambiguity also prompted me to conclude that spirituality must be shaped from within, and not simply assimilated from the spiritual "masters" and "guides." Moreover, it led me to question the wisdom of the "masters" themselves: If they really had been so wise, would the changes have been so radical? The philosophical value of immutability was being challenged by a contrary value: Change is a natural and essential part of growth—a truly wise person is one who recognizes this.

If centuries-old customs, tradition, and spirituality could undergo such a massive transformation, then everything was open to question, including all traditional notions of priesthood and authority. The post-Vatican II era became a time of radical experimenation. The Haight-Ashbury flower children proclaimed love and sexual freedom, while smoking grass and dropping acid. Priests and nuns were encouraged to value and love their feelings, their bodies, their communities, and their world. Many shed their religious garb, redefined their constitutions, initiated ecumenical dialogue, and began immersing themselves in nearly all aspects of social and political work.

During this profound paradigmatic shift, I completed the philosophy studies required of all Jesuits, and began teaching at St. Ignatius High School in San Francisco. I felt far too busy to complain about the loss of the old spirituality or to rejoice in the new. While some Jesuits hated the changes, others embraced them enthusiastically. I felt there was value in both spiritualities—but more than anything, I sensed that no spirituality was perfect.

The first startling setback to the Vatican II's "open window" reform came with Pope Paul VI's encyclical on birth control.

HUMANAE VITAE

Even though this encyclical advanced the worthy thesis that all human life, including embryonic and fetal life, is sacred, it argued that all forms of birth control, except abstinence, were immoral. This teaching was met with an immediate outcry from theologians, priests, and especially married Catholics, who complained that the encyclical created rifts in their marriages by interfering with conjugal intercourse, and with their responsibilities as parents to be good providers for their children.

Prior to the issuance of the encyclical, the pope had appointed a pontifical commission to examine the morality of birth control. The commission's majority opinion was that some forms of birth control, in addition to abstinence, would be morally acceptable. Paul VI chose to reject that majority opinion.

I was aware that the pontifical commission had reached this conclusion, and even though I agreed with them, I did not want to challenge the authority of the pope. I reasoned that the matter, especially for some who had not even completed theological studies, was far too complex to warrant any comment from me.

THE VIETNAM WAR

In the early stages of the conflict, many priests and nuns joined in protest marches and demonstrations against the war. Some bishops, on grounds that the war was just, and that it was totally inappropriate for clergy and sisters to take sides on a political issue, strictly forbade this activity. Defying the ban in the name of conscience and moral obligation, priests were suspended and nuns were forced out of their communities. It disturbed me that religious would be disobedient; but it was also disquieting to realize that bishops who supported the war would demand that the priests and sisters who didn't remain silent.

For years, I wrestled with this dilemma. By the time I finally decided to join in the marches, it was already fashionable to do so. By then, even bishops were demonstrating.

THE VATICAN DECLARATION ON THE ADMISSION OF WOMEN TO THE MINISTERIAL PRIESTHOOD

As mentioned in chapter 6, this Vatican Declaration presented arguments from Scripture and tradition supporting the exclusion of women from the priesthood. Once again, many theologians and others raised their voices in objection. The theologians were reprimanded for their conduct; some of them even had their teaching offices removed.

By this time (1974) I had received a Ph.D. from the Graduate Theological Union in Berkeley and an M.A. in Communications from Loyola Marymount University. I strongly agreed with many of the objections to the declaration. But when all this happened, I was working with Chicano street gangs in East Los Angeles; I was afraid that if I raised my voice in objection, there would be reprisals against me and that I would be ordered to give up my ministry to Chicano youth. So, I said nothing.

DILEMMA REGARDING SOLEMN VOWS

In 1978, after I had finally looked back with careful scrutiny over the previous sixteen years, I felt embarrassed and ashamed. I realized that, out of fear, I had refused to become involved with important matters affecting the welfare of the Church. This fear was generated by the pastoral conflicts mentioned above, and by infrequent personal instances in which superiors' requests seemed either unreasonable or insensitive. (One such instance involved two persons, both claiming to speak in Christ's name, telling me to act in two contradictory fashions to the same situation.)

As closely as I could discern it at the time, the main reason for hesitating to make a solemn promise to be obedient was that I was afraid a superior, in the "name of Christ," might command me to do something I thought was wrong; or, conversely, that a superior, again in the "name of Christ," might forbid me from doing something I felt in conscience obliged to do.

This dilemma presented both moral and philosophical problems. Morally, one is obliged to follow one's conscience; however, some Church authorities would say, "Yes, but not when individual conscience contradicts Church teaching or Church authority." Philosophically, how can two persons, both promising to seek and do God's will, be in opposition?

It became imperative to resolve this dilemma. From that time forward I decided to put off final vows until I had discovered what obedience meant, not only in theory, but in practice.

Over the next seven years I read numerous books and articles on the themes of priesthood, authority, and Jesuit vows. In addition to ongoing conversations with my spiritual advisor, I asked Jesuit superiors and others to explain their understanding of obedience. In particular, I asked them if obedience meant first and foremost loyalty to Vatican teaching, or loyalty to God and the truth. If the latter, was it not a Jesuit's responsibility, therefore, to speak out when Vatican pronouncements violated the truth or God's will? To give precision to this question, I cited the specific instance of the Vatican statement that it "would be difficult to see in a woman at the altar, the image of Christ." I told the superiors that I found this statement theologically erroneous, offensive to the dignity of women, and contrary to the spirit of Christ. And in light of the fact that this Vatican Declaration was disseminated via press releases for the whole world to hear, would not a truly obedient Jesuit raise his voice in public protest so that at least some would know that not everyone in the Church agreed with this declaration?

During that period, the information I gathered from research and personal conversations became increasingly disquieting. I realized that even Jesuit provincials radically disagreed on what obedience meant and how it should be exercised in the specific instance mentioned above. Facts about the dark side of the Church and the priesthood began to emerge—about the massive departures from the priesthood and religious life because of conflicts with authority and celibacy, and about Rome's attempts to forestall, control, and even deny this exodus. During many courses in ecclesiastical history, I learned about the serious failures of Church leaders whose thirst for power or whose lust had done great harm. But these "confessions" were presented as the failures of individuals, not as flaws in the very structure of the Church. It is very telling that in eleven years of Jesuit education, not one teacher or a single textbook ever hinted that the celibacy canons had been forcibly imposed on married priests. I was stunned by the knowledge that a canonical injustice undermining the marriage bond and the priesthood was still wreaking havoc after seventeen centuries.

By 1985, I felt immersed in the Church's failures and sinfulness. But I also realized to a degree never before experienced how much of my own identity was intimately bound up with that same Church: I felt that I was a part of her and she a part of me— virtues, vices, and all. Recognizing my hesitation regarding obedience, the Jesuit Provincial asked me to make a retreat in order to decide once and for all whether I would take solemn vows.

Two other events occurred in 1985 that were to have a profound influence on my life: my brother's death from cancer and meeting Pamela Shoop. These and other personal matters are narrated in considerable detail in another book. Suffice to say here that all the previous years of inquiry, coupled with an awareness of my own past failures and my love for the priesthood and the Church, at last led me to the conviction that obedience meant following the truth, regardless of the cost.

I designed a survey that incorporated in four questions the issues I had been wrestling with for so many years, and which seemed to be of such vital concern to the future of the Church—authority, and whether the priesthood would be more consonant with Christ's teachings and the pastoral needs of the Church by including women as well as men, married as well as celibate.

Instinctively, I believed that the Jesuit superiors then in office would not allow me to speak the truth of what I knew. In November 1985, I wrote a letter to the California Provincial informing him of my decision to resign from the Jesuit Order. He said he was stunned, and suggested I meet with him in person to review my decision. During a November 25th meeting, we discussed once again our differences regarding the meaning of loyalty and obedience in the Society. I showed him the bishops' survey I was working on and said the results might lead to conclusions that would challenge current Vatican policy on the priesthood. I said I felt obedience would obligate me to be truthful to the data, even though it might be at variance with what the pope wanted. Contrary to what he had stated in previous conversations, the Provincial replied, "The Jesuits have always been on the cutting edge. The pope doesn't expect us to simply repeat what he says. He expects us to challenge him. . . ." With this unpredictable reversal, and the promise it held out that obedience was, indeed, loyalty to the truth and to God, I rescinded my decision to resign and energetically pursued the research.

Three weeks after that meeting, the Provincial telephoned. Even though survey results were still coming in, and I had neither written nor revealed anything about the data, he ordered me in the name of Christ, and under threat of dismissal from the Jesuits, to "cease, desist, and destroy" all of my research. I replied that to follow his directive would be to "dishonor the virtue of obedience." That was December of 1985. A month later, I moved out of the Jesuit community.

The next six months were spent finalizing the results of the survey and appealing to the Sacred Congregation for Religious in Rome. I also contacted bishops across the country to ask them if they would accept me as a priest in their diocese. The appeal to Rome was denied. The Jesuit Provincial wrote me a certified letter informing me that my Jesuit vows had been abrogated, that I was suspended as a priest until a bishop would accept me, and that I was still bound by celibacy. The bishops refused to incardinate me, that is, grant me canonical faculties to minister as a priest in their diocese.

In July 1986, on Vocation Sunday, I gave a sermon to the parishioners in a church where I had ministered for six years. The sermon outlined the declining numbers of priests and seminarians, and suggested that one way to resolve the crisis was for the Church to do a thorough and honest review of the celibacy canons, in their origins, history, and present-day practice. Afterward, the pastor told me I was no longer welcome or needed to assist at his parish.

On August 15, 1986, shortly after sending the first draft of the survey results to Pope John Paul II, I signed the final papers of separation from the Jesuit Order. About two months later, Archbishop Mahony of Los Angeles, who had previously refused to incardinate me, offered to grant me temporary faculties as a priest, provided that I help him with the media coverage of the upcoming papal visit, and at the same time set aside my research and avoid all contact with the press. I declined, however, deeming it totally inappropriate to make sacramental ministry contingent upon my compliance with such considerations.

Several months after that, I concluded the first draft of chapter 5 of this book. Data gathered during my eight-year investigation had finally convinced me that the laws binding priests to celibacy were unethical, disordered, and harmful to the Church. Because of the serious implications of this research, I forwarded copies of it to Archbishop Mahony, to the head of the U.S. National Conference of Catholic Bishops, to the apostolic delegate, and to the pope. Months passed, with no comment on my research, no rebuttal, no confirmation.

By the time this phase of the research had been completed, I realized, beyond the fact that the celibacy laws were unjust and unethical, that the pope and other key bishops to whom I had sent my research results either disagreed vehemently, or were indifferent or else afraid; and that any change regarding the laws would need to come from individual priests with the courage to act publicly on their convictions.

This awareness brought with it a radical freedom fully to explore, with Pamela Shoop, the opportunity to love someone as a friend, as an intimate companion, and as a spouse. On November 15, 1987, nearly three years after we had been introduced, Pamela and I were married in the Episcopal Church of St. Matthew. Through joy and pain came clarity. Love is an incredible gift from God, and I realized then that the priesthood benefits greatly in it.

A few weeks after our wedding, Mary Fischer, a journalist who was writing an article for *People* magazine about Pamela and me, called to tell me about her conversation with the personal secretary to the apostolic nuncio in Washington, D.C. She had asked him, "What is Fr. Sweeney's current status as a priest?" Among other things, the reply was, "He has violated the solemn vow of celibacy. He has entered into an invalid union and is in the state of mortal sin. . . ." Assisted by the legal counsel of Bostwick & Ackerman, I wrote a telegram and a detailed letter to the editors of *People* explaining why I thought the comments libelous. They did not publish the article, and the nuncio's office wrote me an apology.

Since my marriage, I have several times been encouraged by friends and officials within the Episcopal Church and other denominations to consider serving them as a priest. Even though I feel profoundly grateful to the Episcopal Church, and sense that we are one in faith, I know that God wants me to remain loyal to the Church in which I was ordained. Although I am canonically suspended from the ministry, I feel that my ministry now is to say what I have learned about authority and the priesthood, and how our Church needs to be radically reformed if we are to survive.

My wife and I joined the national organization of married priests called CORPUS, and we also serve as directors for Good Tidings, a group that ministers to priests and women in love. Because of this, in the past four years we have learned so much about that frightened, immature, and sexually repressed side of the Church; about its fear of love; and about its obstinence and arrogance in maintaining a man-made discipline at the expense of everything else, including the good of the Church and God's will.

Not long after our wedding, Archbishop Mahony wrote me a letter informing me that I was banned from Communion, and would continue to be banned for as long as I continued in my "irregular canonical marriage."

With the advice of Fr. James Coriden, one of the leading canon lawyers in the United States and past president of the Canon Law Society of America, I appealed the ban to Rome. Both Fr. Coriden and I were convinced, in light of the 1983 canon stating that priests who marry without permission are suspended but not excommunicated, that Archbishop Mahony had superceded his authority. The Apostolic Signatura, to whom we had appealed, referred the case to the Sacred Congregation for Priests. Rome upheld the archbishop's ban, however.

For my part, it took only a few seconds to decide whether to "obey" the archbishop's ban. During Mass, I looked up at the altar and asked the Lord: Do you want me not to come? In an image that was not an image, and in words that were not words but heard only in the heart of faith—I saw him stretch out his arms to me and say, "Come."

In 1990, I completed part four of my research on the North American bishops' attitudes on priestly ministry. And in the spring of 1991, my wife and I completed the second draft of a book on how we met and fell in love. Both in that book and in this, it is hoped that our reflections will help the Church to grow less fearful of a priesthood that reveals the feminine and the sacred mysteries of conjugal love, and to grow more eager to embrace that radically free obedience of Jesus, who, standing before the authority of the Holy City and the power of Rome, chose to die rather than to deny the truth.

Appendix A

Sample Letters Regarding Suppression of Research, Resignation from the Jesuits, Priestly Suspension, and Being Banned from Communion

From 1986 through 1991, in correspondence totaling some one hundred and fifty pages, I tried to inform Vatican officials and other members of the hierarchy of the crisis facing the priesthood and Church authority. The correspondence, which included the first draft of chapters 2, 4, and 5 of this volume, attempted to point out that this is not only a pastoral and ideological crisis, it is ethical and theological as well. The Vatican's response to this has been either silence, assertion of its authority, or confirmation of the sanctions imposed for refusing to destroy research and refusing to abide by the ethically dubious canons mandating celibacy. Not once during that five-year period did the Vatican respond directly to any of the ethical or pastoral issues raised. Given the vast administrative responsibilities of the Vatican, silence alone would not have surprised me, but it seems only right that if there is time to punish, there ought to be time to explain why.

It was the Synod on Priestly Formation and the closing remarks of Pope John Paul II that demonstrated very clearly that the Holy See, in the face of worldwide petition, will not even consider a priesthood that includes women or marriage.

Perhaps there was a time when this kind of "authority" was acceptable. However, one need look no further than to the collapse of the Church's seventy-year-old nemesis, the Soviet Union, in order to realize that this kind of power is no longer sustainable and that it has nothing to do with the Man who humbled himself to become one of us. When Vatican authority uses Christ's name to set itself above the people and to demand obedience from them, only two outcomes are possible: idolatry or revolution.

The events behind my correspondence with the Society of Jesus and the Church hierarchy are related in the Epilogue and elsewhere in this volume. Demands of space and other considerations militate against my including all the letters here. The few that are included will hopefully represent, by specific examples, the kind of authority exercised by the Vatican.

THE JESUIT COMMUNITY
LOYOLA MARYMOUNT UNIVERSITY

February 15, 1986

Very Reverend Father Kolvenbach
Curia of the Society of Jesus
Borgo S. Spirito 5
00193 Rome, Italy

Dear Father Kolvenbach: Greetings and Peace

Two days ago I had an extended phone conversation with Fr. Joe Whelan
concerning the unusual, and, in my opinion, unjust circumstances
prompting my resignation from the Jesuit Order.

I am enclosing a copy of the letter I wrote to my Jesuit Community
at Loyola. This letter summarizes the immediate circumstances
leading up to my departure from the Society. I am sending this letter
to you not with the intention of influencing your decision or with
the thought of rescinding my letter of resignation. Rather, it is my
hope that you will pray and reflect on the abuse of authority and
obedience evidenced in this whole matter, and the harm such exercise of
authority brings to individual vocations, the Society, and the Church.

For my own peace of soul -- should you choose to respond -- I would
like to know why you thought my Survey on Priestly Ministry would
bring "great harm to the Society and the Church."

For my part, I love the priesthood and the Society, and the Survey
was part of an attempt to further reflection and discussion
on possible ways to address the current crisis. Over 50% of the
United States Bishops responded to the Survey. Some persons in
authority were upset with the Survey and, through you, tried to stop
it. This kind of silencing seems to me to be detrimental to the
future of Priestly Ministry and an insult to the Bishops and Cardinals
responding to the Survey. If my judgment in this matter is wrong,
I would like to know why.

May the Lord bless you with wisdom and courage to guide the Society
in the footsteps of her Companion and Brother.

In Domino,

Fr. Terry Sweeney

CURIA PRÆPOSITI GENERALIS
    SOCIETATIS IESU
  ROMA · Borgo S. Spirito, 5

March 6, 1986

Rev. Terrance A. Sweeney
c/o P.O. Box 45041
Los Angeles, Calif. 90045

Dear Father Sweeney:

I am replying to your letter of 15 February 1986.

You wrote me in order to give me a copy of the letter you wrote to the Jesuit community at Loyola Marymount University, and I want to acknowledge that enclosure now.

You also wrote, indicating a desire to know why I thought your survey would be harmful. I regret to write that I do not think that I can give you further assistance. As I reflect upon your actions in the light of Jesuit obedience and about the Society's way of proceeding with regard to Church teaching and discipline, and as I consider the scientific quality of the instrument used for the survey, I do not see that I can helpfully add anything to what Father John Clark has already said to you.

I offer you my sincere best wishes, Father Sweeney, and an assurance of my prayers.

In Our Lord,

Peter-Hans Kolvenbach, S.J.

THE CALIFORNIA PROVINCE OF THE SOCIETY OF JESUS

300 College Avenue
P.O. Box 519
Los Gatos, California 95031

March 7, 1986

Terrance A. Sweeney
446 N. Palm Drive
Beverly Hills, California   90210

Dear Terry:

In a recent mailing from Father General, Peter-Hans Kolvenbach, S.J., I received authorization to extend to you the dismissal from the Society which you requested. I am sorry that circumstances brought us to this point.

Your talents and presence among the Jesuits of the California Province are respected and deeply appreciated, Terry. There may have been moments in the past when, on the surface, that was not evident. Yet, I want you to know that never for a moment did words or events lessen our gratutide for the gift you are for the Kingdom.

This notification frees you from the obligation of religious vows. But you remain a priest bound by celibacy who may not exercise priesthood until a bishop receives you. If I can help you in any way to find diocesan placement, please do not hesitate to call on the Provincial Office. Certainly, documentation noting your release from the Society will be necessary before you can begin such a process. Therefore, I am sending it along with the other usual dismissal papers to Bob Caro at LMU. Please give him a call at
     and arrange for a convenient time to sign them and take care of this matter. I spoke with Bob, delegated him to attend to these procedures, and told him to expect to hear from you soon.

You have a special place in my heart and in my prayers, Terry, especially at the Eucharist. Please continue to pray for me.

Yours sincerely in the Lord,

John W. Clark, S.J.
Provincial

cc: Reverend Robert V. Caro, S.J.

ARCHDIOCESE OF LOS ANGELES
1531 WEST NINTH STREET
LOS ANGELES, CALIFORNIA 90015-1194
(213) 251-3288

Office of the Archbishop

May 13, 1986

Reverend Terrence Sweeney
446 North Palm Drive
Beverly Hills, CA 90210

Dear Father Sweeney:

I wish to acknowledge your letter of May 2, 1986 in which you request to
be incardinated in the Archdiocese of Los Angeles.

After consultation and reflection, I am writing to inform you that this
request will not be granted.

I believe that you need to continue working with your spiritual director
and other advisors to discern what the Lord is calling you to do as a
priest within his Church.

Assuring you of my prayers and with every best wish, I am

Sincerely yours in Christ,

+ Roger Mahony

Most Reverend Roger Mahony
Archbishop of Los Angeles

cc: Father John Clark, S.J.
      Provincial

eb

FATHER TERRY SWEENEY
446 NORTH PALM DRIVE
BEVERLY HILLS, CALIFORNIA 90210

May 22, 1986

Cardinal Jean Jerome Hamer, O.P.
Prefect, Sacred Congregation for Religious
3 Piazzo Pio XII
Vatican City, Italy 00193

Your Eminence:

Thank you for accepting my phone call today concerning my
appeal to the Sacred Congregation. I am sorry if the call
inconvenienced you in any way -- I had phoned Rome three-
times earlier before finally reaching you. The person
who answered my third phone call told me to call you
around 6:30 P.M (Rome time), and left a specific number.
I did not know this number was not in your office.

I did not think the matter of my appeal could be handled
over the phone, that is why I asked you if it would
be helpful that I come to Rome and present my case in
person. Since you made it very clear that such a trip
would not be helpful, I will forego consideration of
a personal presentation of my appeal.

You said that my appeal "will be examined in the classical
terms of religious obedience." The letter I sent to you,
dated May 3, presents the details of my situation. But I
want to express to you, briefly and clearly, why I could
not in conscience follow the order of my Jesuit Provincial.

On November 25, 1985, my Provincial, after reading my
cover letter and survey concerning Priestly Ministers,
encouraged me to go forward with the research, even though
I had explicitly stated that the questions were delicate,
that some people may object to them, and that the results
of the research might suggest conclusions which would take
issue with current Church policy. I explicitly asked him
if I was being loyal and obedient in pursuing this specific
research. And he explicitly encouraged me to go forward
with the research.

Three weeks later, he phoned me and ordered me "to cease and
desist" all work on the survey, and to "destroy" the
information I had gathered. I told him I had received
responses from over 100 members of the Hierarchy, and that
to destroy their responses was very serious matter.
Later, after serious prayer and reflection, I felt it would
be <u>wrong</u> to do what the Provincial was asking. He told me

I was placing my judgement over the judgement of Superiors.
He informed me that if I did not follow his order he would
ask me to leave the Society.

I appeal to you: How can I, in conscience, obey the order
of a Superior when that order would have me neglect and
abandon over 100 Bishops' reflections and conclusions
about vital issues affecting Priestly Ministry?

To obey that order would be to betray the minds of the
Bishops, and would be a violation of my conscience,
and a violation of Canons 748.1 and 212.3.

Since my life and priesthood are in considerable turmoil
since the Provincial's ultimatum, and my moving out of
the Jesuit Community after 23 years, I would deeply
appreciate prompt consideration of my appeal.

Thank you for your consideration.

Praying for God's Wisdom --

Fr. Terry Sweeney

CONGREGATIO
PRO RELIGIOSIS
ET INSTITUTIS SAECULARIBUS

Rome, May 26, 1986

Prot. n. 12172/86

Dear Father Sweeney,

The Congregation for Religious and for Secular Institutes has received your appeal for a just and fair judgment on a formal order given you by the Provincial Superior of the California Province of the Society of Jesus.

After careful examination of all the documentation which you sent, this Congregation retains that the Provincial was justified in asking you to "cease and desist" from a public process of taking a poll on four issues on which the Holy See's position is very clear.

Your appeal cannot be upheld because your actions do not conform with the Society's regard for Church teaching nor with Jesuit obedience which "receives its command just as if it were coming from Christ our Savior" since Jesuit obedience is "to one in His place" (Con. 547).

Regrettably, in refusing to obey you have made a clear choice between your research project and your Jesuit vocation.

With a prayer that you may receive light and peace, I am

Faithfully in Christ,

+V. Fagrolo
seer.

Reverend Terry Sweeney
446 North Drive
Beverly Hills, California 90210

U.S.A.

THE CALIFORNIA PROVINCE OF THE SOCIETY OF JESUS
JESUIT PROVINCIAL RESIDENCE

300 College Avenue
P.O. Box 519
Los Gatos, California 95031

(408) 354 6143

July 7, 1986

Terrance A. Sweeney
446 North Palm Drive
Beverly Hills, California 90210

Dear Terry:

As you know, on January 18, 1986, you wrote a letter to the Jesuit Community of Loyola Marymount University announcing your resignation from the Society. As you note, you were resigning because you would not accept my order under holy obedience to cease and desist in your survey of American Bishops on priestly ministers. At the same time you moved from the Jesuit Community at L.M.U. to a private apartment.

You indicated to me you desired to leave the Society voluntarily rather than go through the formal process of dismissal. Accordingly, I prepared forms to facilitate your dismissal, and you acknowledged receipt of these forms on March 11, 1986. I asked you to meet with Father Robert Caro, S.J., Rector of the Jesuit Community of Loyola Marymount, for the signing of these documents. To date you have not done so.

I am now, therefore, writing to repeat, in a formal and solemn manner, my command under holy obedience. This constitutes a first canonical warning and refusal to obey this command will lead to dismissal.

Accordingly, in the name of Our Lord Jesus Christ and in virtue of your vow of obedience, I command you to abandon the aforementioned project immediately and permanently, that you assure me in writing that you have abandoned it and that you will not in any manner whatsoever make the response to your questionnaire which you have or will receive, available to anyone for use in any manner whatsoever.

Furthermore, I hereby warn you that, having carefully listened to the advice of my Consultors, your failure to respond to this command in writing by August 1, 1986, will have as its consequence your dismissal from the Society of Jesus.

Terrance A. Sweeney
July 7, 1986

At this point I must advise you of your right to present to me in writing your reasons for refusing to obey my command, without prejudice however, to the deadline I have set for your response. This is in accord with Canon 697, 2° of the revised Code of Canon Law. I also call your attention to Canon 698 of the new Code where your right to communicate directly with Father General is guaranteed throughout this process.

Terry, I ask that you acknowledge in writing your receipt of this letter. I will remember you, Terry, in my prayers.

Sincerely in Christ,

John W. Clark, S.J.,
Provincial

ARCHDIOCESE OF CHICAGO

POST OFFICE BOX 1979

CHICAGO, ILLINOIS 60690

Office of the Archbishop

August 13, 1986

Dear Father Sweeney:

Thank you for your recent letter in which you indicated your desire to be received as a priest in the Archdiocese of Chicago.

In light of the circumstances described in your letter, in particular your dismissal from the Society of Jesus, it would appear that there are several serious unresolved issues concerning your departure from the Society. Since you write that you are mindful of God's inestimable grace and love shared in the Christian community through the Eucharist, the Sacrament of Reconciliation and prayer, I would encourage you to seek to be reconciled with the Jesuits.

Accordingly, I do not feel it would be in the best interests of either yourself or the Archdiocese for you to be considered for incardination in the Archdiocese of Chicago.

Please be assured of my prayers for a satisfactory resolution of your situation.

With cordial good wishes, I am

Sincerely yours in Christ,

Joseph Card. Bernardin

Archbishop of Chicago

Reverend Terrance A. Sweeney, S.J.
Loyola Marymount University
Loyola Boulevard at 80th Street
Los Angeles, California 90045

cc: Very Reverend John W. Clark, S.J.
     Provincial, California Province of the
        Society of Jesus

OFFICE OF THE VICAR GENERAL

Archdiocese of New York

1011 First Avenue • New York, N.Y. 10022
(212) 371-1000

December 10, 1986

Dear Father Sweeney:

I know that Cardinal O'Connor wrote to you to say I would be in touch with you concerning your request for incardination into the Archdiocese of New York. I apologize for the delay in responding. A number of factors have contributed to the delay.

We have reached the conclusion that it would not be appropriate to proceed with incardination. I have read that Archbishop Mahoney offered assistance. I hope that may be the solution to your present problem.

I am sorry we cannot help. I assure you of my concern and of my prayers.

Sincerely,

+ Joseph T. O'Keefe
Vicar General

Rev. Terrance A. Sweeney
446 N. Palm Drive
Beverly Hills, California 90210

ARCHDIOCESE OF LOS ANGELES
1531 WEST NINTH STREET
LOS ANGELES, CALIFORNIA 90015-1194
(213) 251-3288

January 26, 1988

Office of the Archbishop

Terrance Sweeney
446 North Palm Drive
Beverly Hills, California   90210

Dear Terrance:

When you approached me to receive Holy Communion at our annual Migration Day Mass, celebrated Sunday, January 3, 1988 at Immaculate Conception Church in Los Angeles, I felt compromised in the face of your well-publicized and canonically irregular union, and my own obligation to foster good order within this Archdiocese of Los Angeles.

Among the many duties incumbent upon the Diocesan Bishop is the obligation to promote the common discipline of the whole Church. He is to be watchful lest abuses creep into ecclesiastical discipline, especially concerning the ministry of the Word and the celebration of the Sacraments and Sacramentals.

Keeping in mind the common good of the Church, the rights of others of the faithful, and the duty which we both have toward them, may I ask that you cooperate with me in fulfilling this duty.

Specifically, I ask that you refrain from presenting yourself to me, to my Auxiliary Bishops, or to any priest or minister of the Eucharist within the Archdiocese of Los Angeles, for the reception of the Eucharist for as long as you persist in retaining your present marital status. In the event of a reoccurrence of the incident which provoked this letter, let this letter serve as notice that I, my Auxiliary Bishops, and all priests or ministers of the Eucharist within the Archdiocese of Los Angeles will extend to you a blessing only.

With every best wish, I am

Sincerely yours in Christ,

+ Roger Mahony
Most Reverend Roger Mahony
Archbishop of Los Angeles

j

cc: Auxiliary Bishops, Deans of the Archdiocese

July 1, 1989

PROT. N. 186041/I
(In responso hic numerus referatur)

Rev. Terrance A. Sweeney
3935 Benedict Canyon Drive
Sherman Oaks, California 91423

Dear Rev. Sweeney:

This is in reply to your letters addressed to this Congregation and the documentation regarding your case which has been forwarded to us by the Supreme Tribunal of the Apostolic Signatura "pro competentia".

This Dicastery concurs with what has been written to you by Archbishop Roger Mahony on January 26, 1988, namely that you refrain from presenting yourself for the reception of the Eucharist for as long as you persist in retaining your well-publicized and canonically irregular marital status.

After consultation with members of the Jesuit community in Los Angeles and others, Archbishop Mahony, as diocesan bishop, felt that he had no option but to implement authentic Church doctrine and discipline.

With every best wish, I remain

Faithfully in Christ,

F

Appendix B

Closing Address at the First National Conference on a Married Priesthood

On June 17–19, 1988, at the American University in Washington, D.C., an amazing gathering took place. For the first time in United States Catholic Church history, over 400 married Roman Catholic priests and their wives assembled to discuss the future of the priesthood in the Catholic Church. At this historic conference, sponsored by CORPUS (Corps of Reserve Priests United for Service), men and women shared their stories; their insights; their rejections from families, bishops, and parishes; their personal journeys in faith; their heartaches and happinesses; their children; and their love and hope for the Church. In the midst of much laughter and tears, a profound awakening swept through this unusual and unorthodox gathering. People there began to realize, as a newly assembled community, where the Spirit was leading the Church—toward a priesthood that fully images Christ and God, toward a priesthood that is married and celibate, female and male.

People there realized that great changes in the Church rarely come without great sacrifice, and that the Spirit was calling them to witness to their priesthood and their conjugal love. This witness and this sacrifice would be the cross that would carry the Church in the twenty-first century to a new resurrection.

Women present spoke fearlessly and lovingly of their call to be priests, wives, mothers, and witnesses to the gospel. Married priests whose conjugal love had been spurned and termed "scandalous" forgave their detractors. Wives of priests comforted and supported one another. One priest commented that he had not felt such joy and outpouring of the Spirit since the convening of the Second Vatican Council.

What follows is the closing address that I gave at this first National Conference on a Married Priesthood.

THE SPIRIT OF THE LORD

Jesus, with the power of the Spirit in him, returned to Galilee; and his reputation spread throughout the countryside. He taught in their synagogues and everyone praised him.

He came to Nazareth, where he had been brought up, and went into the synagogue on the sabbath as he usually did. He stood up to read, and they handed him the scroll of the prophet Isaiah. Unrolling the scroll he found the place where it was written: "The spirit of the Lord has been given to me, for he has anointed me. He has sent me to bring good news to the poor, to proclaim liberty to captives, and to the blind new sight, to set the downtrodden free, to proclaim the Lord's year of favor."

He then rolled up the scroll, gave it back to the assistant, and sat down. And all eyes in the synagogue were fixed on him. Then he began to speak to them, "This text is being fulfilled today even as you listen." And he won the approval of all, and they were astonished by the gracious words that came from his lips.

They said, "Is not this Joseph's son?" But he replied, "No doubt you will quote me the saying, 'Physician, heal yourself' and tell me, 'We have heard all that happened in Capernaum, do the same here in your own countryside.' " And he went on, "I tell you solemnly, no prophet is ever accepted in his own country. There were many widows in Israel, I can assure you, in Elijah's day, when heaven remained shut for three years and six months and a great famine raged throughout the land, but Elijah was not sent to any one of these: he was sent to a widow at Zarephath, a Sidonian town. And in the prophet Elisha's time there were many lepers in Israel, but none of these was cured, except the Syrian, Naaman."

When they heard this everyone in the synagogue was enraged. They sprang to their feet and dragged him out of the town, and they took him up to the brow of the hill their town was built on, intending to throw him down the cliff. . . . (Lk. 4:14–30)

What an incredible story: a man who was received with praise, anticipation, enthusiasm; a man who inspired and delighted his listeners, was, within minutes, swept up in a rage, dragged to the brow of a hill by a riotous mob of worshipers to be thrown over the cliff to his death.

What prompted this sudden, radical reversal from thoughts of praise to actions of murder? The hardness of men's hearts colliding with the Spirit of the Lord, the Spirit of truth who knows and lays bare the secret thoughts of all. And what saving truth did the Spirit prompt Jesus to proclaim to that group in that synagogue who rejoiced in that scriptural promise of salvation, yet doubted how a son of Joseph, their neighborhood carpenter, could have any significant role in such fulfillment? Jesus uttered a twofold truth: The Israelites doubted, rejected, scorned, and killed the prophets before him; God loves the Gentiles.

They wanted to kill him for this, the very truth whose acceptance would have led to their salvation. Jesus was telling them: Your faith is weak and blind. You scorn your prophets. God loves your enemies. The Spirit of the Lord is proclaiming the good news to the Gentiles. The Spirit of the Lord is setting your enemies free. The Spirit of the Lord is giving sight to the Gentiles. O, how the words must have burned in their ears; O, the wrath they must have felt.

Now, 2,000 years later, Father's Day, 1988, what is the Spirit saying through this body of women and children, married and celibate priests, gathered in a basement of a Methodist university in the freedom capital of the world? What is the Spirit saying through you wives who have been told your love is a sin? And you fathers who have been forbidden by law ever to father while remaining a father? The Spirit of the Lord, through you, is proclaiming a two-fold truth: God loves woman; Jesus, in his wisdom, called and is calling married and celibate, female and male to be his disciples.

It is a sign of the darkness of the times that for this truth you are being scorned, cajoled, repudiated, vilified, and excommunicated. It is a sign of the darkness of the times that for following that whisper of the Spirit in your hearts—God is love, and he who loves is born of God and knows God, for God is love; for living that radical teaching of Christ—the Sabbath was made for man, not man for the Sabbath—you are being wrenched away from your priesthood or from the woman or man you love. It is through your witnessing to this truth that the Spirit has led you into the very heart of Christ, the prophet who cried out to his Church: "O Jerusalem, Jerusalem . . . how often have I longed to gather your children, as a hen gathers her chicks under her wings, and you refused!" And like Christ the prophet, this truth is leading you to the cross, the cross that pits man against woman, conjugal love against celibate love.

God loves woman: Jesus, in his wisdom, called and is calling married and celibate, female and male to be his disciples. God, who is wisdom, God who is life, God who is generative love said: Let us make man in our own image. . . . In his own image he created them. To be woman is to be the very image of God. To be woman is to be wisdom, life, procreative love. To be woman is to cause God to exclaim: All that I have created is good. To be woman is to cause man to rejoice: Ah, at last, here is flesh of my flesh and bone of my bones; and that is why a man leaves his father and mother and clings to his wife, and the two become one flesh.

To be woman is to hear the Spirit proclaim: Hail, Mary, full of grace, the Lord is with thee. Blessed are you among women, and blessed is the fruit of they womb. To be woman is to say yes and to bear and nurture into the world the body and blood of Jesus. To be woman is to hear: Your child will cause the rise and fall of many, and your own soul a sword shall pierce. To be woman is to be an infidel and yet still believe that Jesus can heal my daughter. To be woman is to have a flow of blood and to believe that in merely touching the hem of his garment I will be healed. To be woman is to have five husbands, yet still to thirst, still to seek the truth, still to long for God, still to proclaim the wisdom of Jesus. To be woman is to have sinned, yet still to fall at the feet of Jesus and anoint his feet with oil, with tears, with your hair. To be woman is to stand at the foot of the cross throughout his agony, to go to the tomb to touch his dead body, to proclaim to the fear-ridden, despairing apostles: He is risen!

It was not the Spirit of the Lord who said: Woman, thy name is evil. It was not the Spirit of the Lord who said: It would be hard to see in a woman at the altar the person of Christ. It was not the Spirit of the Lord who said: There were no women at the Last Supper. It was not the Spirit of the Lord who said: The Church has never ordained women.

The Spirit of the Lord did say: "Who is my mother? Who are my brothers? . . . Anyone who does the will of my Father in heaven, he is my brother and sister and mother." With these words and in his actions Jesus proclaimed forever that flesh and blood and gender are not the cause of communion or separation, and never should be the reason for discrimination or exclusion. To exclude human beings from the priesthood solely on the basis that they are women is a scandal, an affront, a violation of the Spirit of Jesus, a violation of nature, both human and divine. This scandal divides woman from man, woman from Christ, woman from her own Godliness, her wisdom, her life, her creative love. This scandal tears asunder the one Body of Christ.

It was the Spirit who prompted Jesus to choose both married and unmarried to be his disciples. It was the Spirit who prompted Jesus to say to a married man: "Blessed are you, Simon, son of John! Because it was not flesh and blood that revealed this to you but my Father in heaven. So now I say to you: You are Peter and on this rock I will build my Church."

It was the Spirit who prompted Jesus to love the law and to proclaim: I have come not to abolish the law, but to fulfill it. It was the Spirit who prompted that same Jesus to break the law, to heal on the Sabbath, and to finally proclaim that statement which led to his death: The Sabbath was made for man, not man for the Sabbath.

It was the Spirit that prompted Jesus to say: What God has joined, let no man divide. It was the Spirit that prompted Paul to say: In my opinion, it is better for a man not to marry, in order to be free for prayer; but I'm telling you from the Lord: It is wrong for a husband to put away his wife, or for a wife to leave her husband. And if you decide to be continent in order to pray, do so for only a short, mutually agreed time, lest the devil tempt you. And beware of those who say marriage is forbidden; such teaching is from the devil. It was not the Spirit of the Lord who prompted the saying: Faced with the purity of Christ's body, all sexual union is impure.

It was not the Spirit of the Lord that prompted the first extant canon regarding continence, a canon imposed on validly married clergy: "Bishops, presbyters, and deacons and all other clerics having a position in the ministry are ordered to abstain completely from their wives and not to have children. Whoever, in fact, does this, shall be expelled from the dignity of the clerical state" (canon 33, Council of Elvira in 306).

It was not the Spirit of the Lord that prompted further canons ordering priests not to sleep in the same bed as their wives, or in the same house. It was not the Spirit that prompted numerous abuses and hardships inflicted on married priests and their wives, abuses including dismissal from the clerical state, loss of income, public scorn, imposed fasting, scourging, death, and the wives and children of priests —for the "benefit" of the Church—being sold into slavery. These were crimes against humanity and God, who made man and woman to be wisdom, life, love.

It was not the Spirit that prompted Lateran II in 1139 to enact laws ruling all marriages of priests, present and future, invalid. What is the Spirit saying through this body? That the Body of Christ is one—male and female, married and celibate—and that until the full image of the Body is reflected throughout the entire Church, community and institution, the Church will suffer and die.

What is the Spirit saying to this body? You are the future Church.

You are the Church of the twenty-first century. Your love images the full Christ. And it is precisely because you have listened to the law of love in your hearts, more than any man-made discipline, that you are being nailed to the cross, driven from your communities, scorned, humiliated. It is through your crucifixion, through your love being called a sin, that you have entered into the mystery of Christ the prophet. It is through your listening to the voice of love above any other voice, and through your not abandoning the Church or the priesthood, that the Church of the twenty-first century is being born. Your consciences have been seared. Your love has been mocked. You are the prophets of the Church to come. You are witness to the Church Jesus founded, where married and celibate, female and male were called to be his disciples.

May that same Spirit, who has brought you to the cross of love, help you to realize that your sufferings will give birth to a new resurrection of the Church, the full Body of Christ—female and male, married and celibate—the full body of man and woman, the full image of God, God who is wisdom, God who is life, God who is love.

Bibliography

Aquinas, Saint Thomas. *Summa Theologiae: A Concise Translation.* Edited by Timothy McDermott. London: Eyre and Spottiswoode, 1989.

Audet, J. P. *Structure of Christian Priesthood: Home, Marriage and Celibacy in the Pastoral Service of the Church.* New York: Macmillan, 1968.

Augustine. *Confessions.* Edited and translated by William Watts. London: William Heinemann, 1919.

Bailey, D. *The Man-Woman Relation in Christian Thought.* London: Longmans, Green, 1959.

————. *Sexual Relation in Christian Thought.* New York: Harper & Brothers, 1959.

Barstow, Anne L. *Married Priests and the Reforming Papacy: The Eleventh-Century Debates.* New York: The Edwin Mellen Press, 1982.

Bassett, William, and Peter Huizing, eds. *Celibacy in the Church.* New York: Herder and Herder, 1972.

Boff, Leonardo. *Church: Charism and Power.* New York: Crossroad, 1985.

Brown, Raymond. *The Virginal Conception and Bodily Resurrection of Jesus.* New York: Paulist Press, 1974.

Brown, Raymond; J. Fitzmeyer; and R. Murphy, eds. *The Jerome Biblical Commentary.* Englewood Cliffs, N.J.: Prentice-Hall, 1968.

Bullough, Vern. *Sexual Variance in Society and History.* New York: Wiley Interscience, 1976.

Bullough, Vern, and J. Brundage. *Sexual Practices in the Medieval Church.* Buffalo, N.Y.: Prometheus Books, 1982.

Burghardt, Walter. *Woman: New Dimensions.* New York: Paulist Press, 1977.

Caillau, D. A. B., ed. *Omnia opera.* Paris: Paul Mellier, 1844.

Cochini, Christian. *Origines apostoliques du célibat sacerdotal.* Paris: Lethielleux, 1981.

The Code of Canon Law (in English translation). Grand Rapids: William B. Eerdmans Publishing Company, 1983.

Copleston, F. C. *Aquinas.* Baltimore: Penguin Books, 1955.

Coriden, James. *Sexism and Church Law.* New York: Paulist Press, 1974.

Creighton, M. *A History of the Papacy from the Great Schism to the Sack of Rome.* 5 vols. London: Longmans, Green, 1897.

Danielou, Jean. *The Ministry of Women in the Early Church.* London: Faith Press, 1961.

Daly, Mary. *Beyond God the Father.* Boston: Beacon Press, 1973.

———. *The Church and the Second Sex.* New York: Harper & Row, 1968.

Empie, P., and M. Austin, eds. *Papal Primacy and the Universal Church.* Minneapolis: Augsburg Publishing House, 1974.

Fichter, Joseph H. *America's Forgotten Priests.* New York: Harper & Row, 1968.

Friedberg, E., ed. *Corpus juris canonici.* 2 vols. Leipzig, 1879–1881.

Funk, F. X., ed. *Didascalia et constitutiones apostolorum.* Paderborn, Germany, 1905.

Gardiner, Anne M., ed. *Women and Catholic Priesthood: An Expanded Vision.* New York: Paulist Press, 1976.

Grant, Robert M. *Gnosticism: A Sourcebook of Heretical Writings from the Early Christian Period.* New York: Harper & Bros., 1961.

Greeley, Andrew M., director. *The Catholic Priest in the United States.* Washington, D.C.: Publications Office, United States Catholic Conference, 1972.

Gryson, Roger. *Les origines du célibat ecclésiastique du premier au septième siècle.* Gembloux: J. Duculot, SA., 1970.

―――. *The Ministry of Women in the Early Church.* Translated by Jean Laporte and Mary Louise Hall. Collegeville, Minn.: The Liturgical Press, 1976.

Hasler, A. *How the Pope Became Infallible.* New York: Doubleday, 1981.

Hefele, Carl Joseph. *History of the Christian Councils.* 5 vols. Edinburgh, 1894–1896.

Heyer, R., ed. *Women and Orders.* New York: Paulist Press, 1974.

Jeremias, Joachim. *Jerusalem in the Time of Jesus.* Translated by F. H. Cave et al. Philadelphia: Fortress Press, 1969.

Jonas, Hans. *The Gnostic Religion.* Boston: Beacon Press, 1958.

Jones, Alexander, ed. *The Jerusalem Bible.* Garden City, N.Y.: Doubleday & Co., Inc., 1966.

Kelly, J. N. D. *Early Christian Doctrines.* 2d ed. New York: Harper & Row, 1960.

―――. *Jerome: His Life, Writings, and Controversies.* New York: Harper & Row, 1976.

Ketter, Peter. *Christ and Womankind.* Westminster, Md.: Newman Press, 1952.

Kung, Hans. *Infallible? An Inquiry.* Translated by E. Quinn. New York: Doubleday & Co., 1971.

Laeuchli, S. *Power and Sexuality: The Emergence of Canon Law at the Synod of Elvira.* Philadelphia: Temple Unviersity Press, 1972.

Lea, Henry C. *History of Sacerdotal Celibacy in the Christian Church.* New Hyde Park, N.Y: University Books, 1966.

McKenna, Mary L. *Women in the Church.* New York: P. J. Kenedy & Sons, 1967.

McKenzie, J. L. *Authority in the Church.* New York: Sheed and Ward, 1966.

―――. *Dictionary of the Bible.* Milwaukee, 1968.

Matura, T. *Celibacy and Community: The Gospel Foundations for Religious Life.* Translated by P. Oligny. Chicago: Franciscan Herald Press, 1968.

Metz, J. B. *Followers of Christ: Religious Life and the Church.* Translated by T. Lanton. New York: Paulist Press, 1978.

Moloney, Francis J. *Disciples and Prophets: A Biblical Model for Religious Life.* New York: Crossroad, 1981.

Morris, Joan. *The Lady Was a Bishop: The Hidden History of Women with Clerical Ordination and the Jurisdiction of Bishops.* New York: The Macmillan Co., 1973.

Noonan, John T. *Contraception: A History of its Treatment by the Catholic Theologians and Canonists.* New York: The New American Library, 1967.

Quasten, J., and J. C. Plumpe, eds. *Ancient Christian Writers.* London: Longmans, Green, 1952.

Quinonez, L. A. *Patterns in Authority and Obedience: An Overview of Authority/Obedience Developments Among U.S. Women Religious.* Washington, D.C.: Leadership Conference of Women Religious, 1978.

Rahner, Karl. *The Shape of the Church to Come.* New York: Seabury, 1974.

Raming, I. *The Exclusion of Women from the Priesthood: Divine Law or Sex Discrimination?* Translated by N. Adams. Metuchen, N.J.: Scarecrow Press, 1976.

Ranke-Heinemann, Uta. *Eunuchs for the Kingdom of Heaven.* New York: Doubleday, 1990.

Robinson, James M. *The Nag Hammadi Library in English.* New York: Harper & Row, 1977.

Ruether, Rosemary R. *Sexism and God-Talk: Toward a Feminist Theology.* Boston: Beacon, 1983.

———. *Women–Church.* San Francisco: Harper & Row, 1985.

———, ed. *Religion and Sexism.* New York: Simon and Schuster, 1974.

Schillebeeckx, E. *Celibacy.* New York: Sheed & Ward, 1968.

———. *The Church with a Human Face.* New York: Crossroad, 1985.

Stuhlmueller, C., ed. *Women and Priesthood: Future Directions; A Call to Dialogue from the Faculty of the Catholic Theological Union at Chicago.* Collegeville, Minn.: Liturgical Press, 1978.

Swidler, Leonard. *Women in Judaism: The Status of Women in Formative Judaism.* Metuchen, N.J.: Scarecrow Press, 1976.

Tavard, George. *Woman in Christian Tradition.* South Bend, Ind.: Notre Dame University Press, 1973.

Tennant, F. R. *The Sources of the Doctrine of the Fall and Original Sin.* New York: Schocken Books, 1968.

Thomas, Gordon. *Desire and Denial.* Boston: Little, Brown & Co., 1986.

Van der Meer, H. *Women Priests in the Catholic Church?* Translated by Arlene and Leonard Swidler. Philadelphia: Temple University Press, 1973.

Walzer, R., ed. *Galen on Jews and Christians.* London: Oxford University Press.

Widengren, G. *Mani and Manichaeism.* London: Weidenfeld and Nicolson, 1965.

Women and the Priesthood; A Selected and Annotated Bibliography. Compiled by P. Kendall. The Episcopal Diocese of Pennsylvania: published by the Committee to Promote the Cause of and to Plan for the Ordination of Women to the Priesthood, 1976.

Index